ZOOCHECK CANADA
3266 Yonge Street, Ste. 1417
Toronto, Ontario
Canada, M4N 3P6

LEOPARD IN THE AFTERNOON

AN AFRICAN TENTING SAFARI

CHRISTOPHER ONDAATJE

LESTER & ORPEN DENNYS
PUBLISHERS

FIRST EDITION

Canadian Cataloguing in Publication Data

Ondaatje, Christopher
Leopard in the afternoon

ISBN 0-88619-266-8 (bound) ISBN 0-88619-268-4 (pbk.)

1. Tanzania - Description and travel - 1981- . 2. Serengeti National Park (Tanzania). 3. Photography of animals - Tanzania. 4. Safaris - Tanzania. 5. Ondaatje, Christopher. I. Title.

DT440.5.063 1989 916.78 C89-094433-4

Book design by Jackie Young/ink.
Printed in Canada by General Printers.
Bound in Canada by John Deyell Company.
Project management by Paula Chabanais & Associates.

Published in Canada by
Lester & Orpen Dennys
78 Sullivan Street
Toronto, Canada
M5T 1C1

Acknowledgements

It has been said that all journeys to Africa are the same. It isn't so. They are very different, and I will always be grateful to George Butterfield, who first convinced me to go to Tanzania to see the last great herds of wild animals left in the world.

My thanks also to my daughter Jans, who allowed me to use her photograph of a wet cheetah hunting in the Serengeti, and the final picture of the giraffe mating sequence; to Wayne Todd, a master craftsman in Bermuda, who worked tirelessly with me to get the correct colour tones in the photos for this book; and, of course, to Karen Blixen (Isak Dinesen), Peter Matthiessen, Beryl Markam, Ernest Hemingway, Elspeth Huxley, Laurens van der Post, and Bernhard Grzimek, who were there before me and who certainly showed me the way.

Finally, and most of all, I am grateful to my wife, Valda, who understood my African obsession and gave me so much help and encouragement in a fascinating but difficult editorial project. I could not have written this book without her.

For Valda, David, Sarah, and Jans;
for Liz and Kevin;
and for Alex Brown and Mark Wheeler, who shared the experience.

The black-backed jackal can easily be distinguished by its silvery black saddle. Both predators and scavengers, jackals are noisy members of a pack and scream or howl at each other when a kill is located.

Previous page: In the early sunrise, Mount Meru dominates the horizon. Farther away, in the distance, we could see the giant square-topped cone of Kilimanjaro — symbol of adventure and the highest mountain in Africa. A few minutes later, as the heat increased, the mountain vanished in the haze.

A new-born Thomson's gazelle fawn — the commonest gazelle in East Africa. Female gazelles will sometimes band together to protect their young from predators. The vulnerable fawns can even be taken by the larger birds of prey.

Contents

INTRODUCTION xv

CHAPTER ONE *Arrival* 1

CHAPTER TWO *Down to Lake Natron* 13

CHAPTER THREE *The Second Day* 29

CHAPTER FOUR *Serengeti* 41

CHAPTER FIVE *The Fourth Day* 59

CHAPTER SIX *Lake Ndutu* 75

CHAPTER SEVEN *Ngorongoro Crater* 102

CHAPTER EIGHT *Tarangire* 135

CHAPTER NINE *Maasai Country* 161

CHAPTER TEN *Return to Seronera* 185

EPILOGUE 205

Introduction

In Canto 7 of The Purgatorio *Dante describes in the Valley of the Princes one of his gentlest locales, the habitation of those melancholy rulers who were seduced from their true end by the magnificence of their royal means and are now imprisoned in a gilded imitation of their own gardens.*

LEE PATERSON **Negotiating the Past**

Any profession — whether one is a writer, wrestler, stockbroker, or butcher — comes with a life style. And all of us at some stage tend to get locked within the ceremonies of whatever career we have chosen. At this point the objects around us, the props of our trade, begin to describe us. The decorations in our homes and offices and shops represent us. Like Dante's princes we are known for the portrait of ourselves that is not of our own making.

In *The Unbearable Bassington* by Saki, Francesca Bassington "if pressed in an unguarded moment to describe her soul would probably have described her living room." Saki's satirical arrow hits home as true today as when he first fired it off into the world. That living room, that garden of princes, is what my brother has been escaping from in the last few years. And this is a book about an escape, a renewal — either of stepping back to what one was or stepping forward into a new world. And like other writers and characters in fiction or real life — from Hemingway to Saul Bellow's Henderson — my brother chose Africa as his time machine.

I think most people who know my brother imagine him as an international financier in a pin-striped suit. If they know him better they have witnessed him singing Hoagy Carmichael's "My Resistance is Low", accompanying himself on the guitar. But mostly he is known for what he has done in the last twenty years — which is to battle his way into and build a financial empire, warrior-style.

The brother I first knew was one who loved nature, especially birds. This was as a child in Ceylon and later as a teenager in England. Even then he was a photographer. I still remember a small black-and-white photograph he took with a box camera, through a telescope, of a bird. But that interest went underground for a long time. When I arrived in Canada in 1962, he was already in the world of finance, battling his way in.

He is a private creature. He breasts his cards. And while I knew things were being reshuffled in his life during the last few years and that he was going over to Africa whenever he could, I didn't know what was up. Like most members of our family he likes to do something, make something *completely*, before he returns with it — a song, a deal, a book. In spite of our family's gregariousness, things are done and made alone. We like to learn from strangers — as he does from Joshua and Thad Petersen in this book. So in many ways I come to this book of his as much a stranger as the next person.

There is a moment when he talks about fear.

> *I wasn't frightened. I've never been frightened in situations like that. Nor am I really frightened of dying. But when I'm involved in a project such as this, I'm terrified of dying before I've completed it.*

The fear is not death then, the fear is that a project is unfinished, or in some way that we die incomplete. On another level I think this is what the book is about. My brother had sewn himself into a certain kind of world and he was somehow cutting his way out to enter another side of the world. No one can look at him today and mistake his soul for a living room in Toronto or London.

Now his previous world is left behind and it is a delight to watch him within this new world as he is swallowed into a landscape that is "warm and brown. Hot brown, deep brown, brown brown." He looks at and suddenly notices how incongruous toothpaste is. A new spirit emerges. Seeing flamingoes he says to himself, "I longed to be engulfed in the pink cloud."

There is a constant wry humour in how he describes his safari.

> *Thad and I had two strong glasses of Sundowner gin with tonic before dinner. It practically blew our heads off. The locally brewed or distilled gin was bottled by*

Mahonda Liquors in Zanzibar, under Zanzibar
government supervision, which wasn't much consolation.

And he evokes a texture of place and event — giraffes drinking awkwardly, lion sounds at night. The hyena attack on the camp is a wonderful, abrupt scene, perfectly sketched, as is the wildebeest kill by the lioness. Most of all there is a directness and honesty he reveals which is, in the end, what allows him to change during the course of the book. He admits his desires and emotions — that in Africa he identifies with the predator, not the hunted — also saying, "If I could stay in Africa for an extended period I would study the hyena. His very repellence is fascinating."

There is a precision in the writing and a lack of pretension that makes the record of the journey a pleasure. We are comfortable with him as a fellow traveller, as he draws his self-portrait.

It is an intriguing book, a strange metaphor of self-discovery beneath all the theatre of Africa and travel and photography. I have got to know my brother better because of it. What I like is his directness at times, at times his evasiveness, his humour, his love of the birds and Joshua and the mornings and the breakfasts and the feathery acacias. What I like is that the landscape he chooses for his self-portrait emerges clearly in the writing and photographs. The strange raw beauty of Africa. This is what he discovers.

Landscapes are camouflage for some people. You hug the texture of a place and you hide within it, you learn from it — whether it is a monastery or a school or a stock exchange or a base camp — and then you move on. I think that my brother is still a nomad in some way. Over there! you tell him, pointing, the new world! And he will be off.

Michael Ondaatje

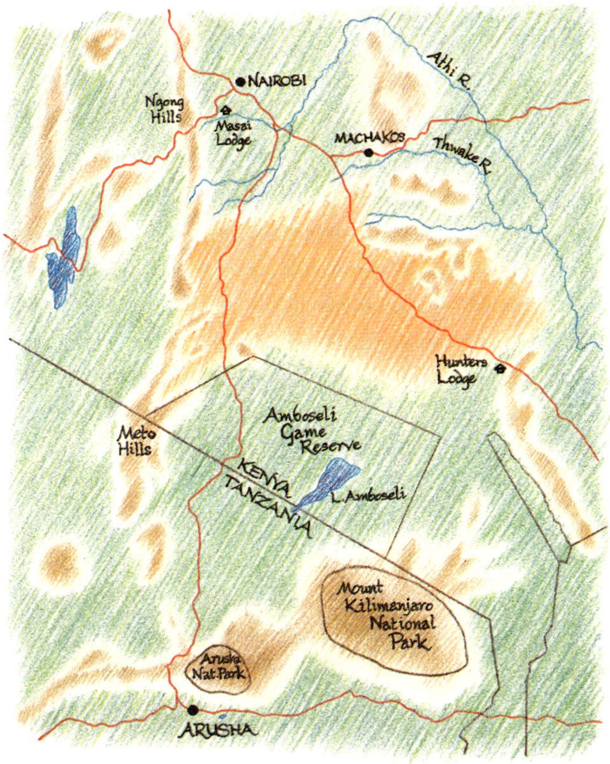

CHAPTER ONE

Arrival

...there are many Africas. There are as many Africas as there are books about Africa — and as many books about it as you could read in a leisurely lifetime. Whoever writes a new one can afford a certain complacency in the knowledge that his is a new picture agreeing with no one else's, but likely to be haughtily disagreed with by all those who believe in some other Africa.

BERYL MARKHAM **West with the Night**

Nairobi at last! I had been travelling for the better part of two days and was numbed into a near stupor by the time changes, the airport waits, the hours of sitting in a plane. I was also full of anticipation, and as I stepped out into the hot, dry, tropical night just after midnight I felt an unexpected sense of *déjà vu,* a sense of recognition. In that brief instant, in the busy African scene just outside the airport, I remembered similar scenes from a time long forgotten. I had spent my early childhood in Ceylon before it was granted its independence by the British in 1948. Now, unexpectedly, reliving old emotions, I suddenly felt I belonged here, and with the feeling came a sense of release, of freedom to seize a new reality.

Nairobi is a modern city not attractive by western standards, a loathsome symbol of the changing Africa. The town that Bror Blixen described in 1913 as nothing but an old anchovy tin is now a sprawling hodgepodge of tall office buildings, shops, and bazaars. It was originally a simple rail depot servicing the railroad linking Kenya's coast to Lake Victoria. Before the railroad and the British came, Africans in the region lived in small settlements scattered around Mount Kenya. Nairobi was merely a swamp that the Africans avoided. The word *N'erobi* itself is a Maasai word meaning "place of cold waters".

In the 1880s and 1890s, Africa was seen by the European powers as a vast and inert prize. Britain, Germany, and France, in particular, were in a headlong scramble to establish areas of control. The Conference of Berlin in 1884–85 attempted to bring order to this mêlée, and Africa was apportioned among the major powers like a Christmas turkey.

Tall, thin, handsome, and proud, the Maasai have so far withstood most western influences and cling to their way of life as warriors and herdsmen.

When Kenya became a British colony at the end of the nineteenth century, it attracted a wide range of white settlers, including many more or less upper-class Englishmen and aristocratic Europeans who gave life in the colonies some panache. Beryl Markham and Karen Blixen were of this world, and that lingering colonial style was very familiar to me from my early childhood in Ceylon.

Germany was established in the part of East Africa known as Tanganyika, which remained a German colony until the First World War. Then it became a British protectorate, largely left to itself, in contrast to Kenya, which was more extensively settled and developed. As a result, there is a greater opportunity in Tanzania of seeing Africa as it was and as it has been for thousands of years. (In 1964 Tanganyika and Zanzibar united to form The United Republic of Tanzania.) Compared to the free-wheeling economy of Kenya, Tanzania has remained desperately poor, and while it has some of the most magnificent game reserves in the world, it simply cannot afford to look after them.

There are many safaris that can be made in East Africa, but I had been encouraged to go to Tanzania to see the last great spectacle of wildlife remaining in the world. My plan was to go on a short tenting safari setting off from Arusha in Tanzania. To get to Arusha it was easiest to go through Nairobi. I set off driving south to the Tanzanian border — a tiring, uncomfortable 125-mile trek.

During the long afternoon drive through dry savannah punctuated by towns consisting almost entirely of small tin wayside shops, my North American world gradually began to recede. I had recently been feeling deeply dissatisfied with my present way of life. For more than a quarter of a century I had pursued financial success with an almost single-minded obsession. In the last five years especially, profits and assets had increased dramatically. But my satisfaction was decreasing proportionately. The original shareholders who had backed my company in its risky early years remained, but a whole new herd of shareholders, lured by the firm's growth, had appeared on the scene to make ever-increasing demands for greater investment to produce still more earnings and still more dividends. I felt I was little more than a slave catering to investors' needs. But though my zest for the financial side of the enterprise was dwindling, I had invested a tremendous amount of intellectual, emotional, and physical energy in it. I had even had dynastic ambitions. I felt pulled in two directions, and my struggle to resolve the conflict had been occupying my mind to the exclusion of all else.

We were speeding into the Africa of tomorrow as the Africa of yesterday looked on: women digging in the fields; boys tending goats and cattle; warriors standing proudly by the roadside; young girls carrying sticks; children playing on side streets; vendors selling trinkets and beads — yesterday's emblems — to anyone not in too much of a hurry to stop and bargain.

There are still more than three hundred thousand Maasai in Kenya and Tanzania, maintaining their ancient culture based on ownership of cattle. It will be difficult for this proud people to preserve their land and customs in the coming years.

I needed a new direction, but so far had found nothing of sufficient magnitude to jolt me out of my preoccupation. Now, however, as I progressed into the vastness of the African landscape, I felt the pressure of my thoughts begin to ease.

> *... until you actually saw it and travelled across it on foot or on horseback or in a wagon, you could not possibly grasp the enormous vastness of Africa. It seemed to go on for ever and ever; beyond each range of hills lay another far horizon; always it was the same, pale-brown grass and bush and thorn-trees, rocky mountains, dark valleys, sunlit plain....*
>
> ELSPETH HUXLEY **The Flame Trees of Thika**

At Namanga on the Kenya-Tanzania border I changed cars and drivers and was driven the remaining fifty miles through more dry, dusty country. No more little tin villages, only the occasional thin proud Maasai herdsman leaning on his stick by the side of the road.

The town of Arusha is dominated by Mount Meru, Tanzania's second highest mountain after Kilimanjaro. Standing just behind Arusha, Meru casts its long shadows on the town. That first evening in Arusha I met and had dinner with the man who was to be my host over the next two weeks, Thad Petersen, and his attractive young American wife, Robin. His father is a Lutheran missionary who has spent the greater part of his life in Tanzania. Petersen was born here when it was still Tanganyika, has lived here most of his life, and has a genuine love and sense of wonder for Africa and the African people. He and his two brothers lead small safaris and walking tours from a base in Arusha. I liked him immediately. Quiet and unpretentious, he is relaxed and casual, not at all the overbearing white hunter in a safari suit that one reads about. He usually wanders around in black handmade tire sandals — almost a trademark with him.

He warned me: "Don't photograph the Maasai or the other Africans. They don't like it unless you ask them. They are very sensitive and think you are taking away part of their soul with the photograph. Also, don't drink the water, unless it's distilled. Otherwise you'll have terrible stomach problems." He also reassured me: "What we're going to try to do is to stay away from people...to tent in maximum freedom, to do what we like with no rigid schedule. This will give you a much more realistic picture of the true Tanzania than you'd otherwise see."

Jet-lagged as hell, desperate to get to bed, I was still full of questions. What chance is there to see lion? Wildebeest migration? Cheetah? The Rift Valley? He assured me, guaranteed me, that there would definitely be lion, several lions, herds of wildebeest. Pretty sure to see cheetah too. What about leopards? He said: "I doubt if you'll see a leopard. They're very shy and extremely difficult to find. But we'll try." I was disappointed — but secretly and immediately I determined to see a leopard.

Unknowingly, Thad had just given me the reason I needed for my journey. A destination, a goal, helps give reason to an adventure, enhances the traveller's enjoyment of the journey. I needed the journey, but I also needed the reason for the journey.

> *A Bushman father, for instance, would never give his son the meat of a jackal to eat because the jackal was a coward and this would make the child cowardly too. He gave the child the heart of a leopard, as he gave its mind the heart of a star, because a leopard was one of the bravest of the brave and would make the child brave.*
>
> LAURENS VAN DER POST **The Heart of the Hunter**

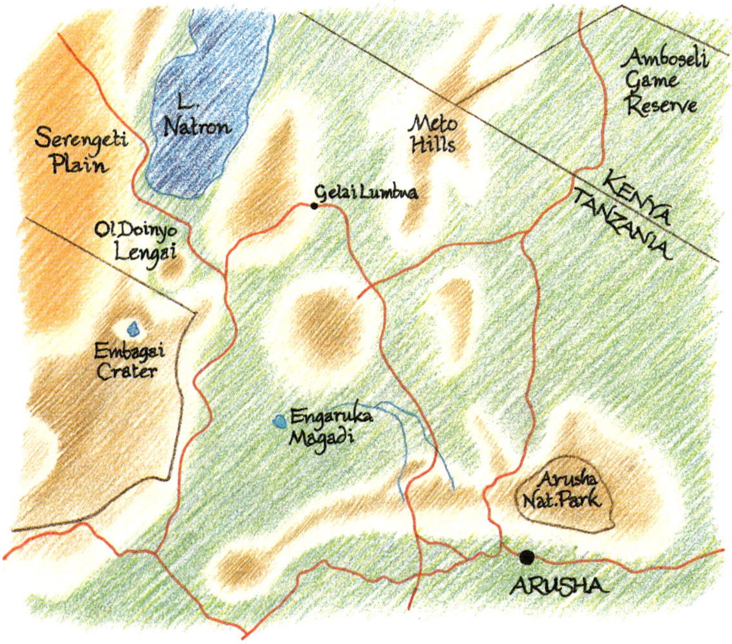

CHAPTER TWO

Down to Lake Natron

Africa is mystic; it is wild; it is a sweltering inferno; it is a photographer's paradise, a hunter's Valhalla, an escapist's Utopia. It is what you will, and it withstands all interpretations. It is the last vestige of a dead world or the cradle of a shiny new one.

BERYL MARKHAM **West with the Night**

Twenty-four hours later I was lying awake on a low canvas cot in a small canvas tent. It was hot, an oppressive dry heat. I tossed and turned my way through the night, listening to a whole symphony of African noises — the distant high-pitched wheezing cry of zebra, the chattering of baboons, the scuttling of small feet near the tent. I could not have been more happy.

Petersen picked me up soon after an early breakfast. He had a Land Rover into which we packed all our luggage and supplies. Petersen drove. It was a bit of a scramble getting out of the hotel in Arusha. There were the usual crowds of tourists, and there was the business of checking out and changing money, all of which he patiently handled. For a hundred dollars I got a whole stack of Tanzanian shillings — five thousand of them. I remember feeling quite embarrassed as I stuffed the huge mass of paper currency into my pocket.

Then we drove off. It was uncomfortable but fascinating right from the first moment — driving through Arusha, seeing the African villagers, some dressed totally in black with white ceremonial paint on their faces. They weren't Maasai, and I learned later they were young Warusha teenagers who had just been proudly initiated in their circumcision ceremony. It was a photographer's paradise, but I remembered Thad Petersen's warning not to photograph people. I desperately wanted to record the colours, the warm tones, and the Gauguin-like postures of the villagers sitting on the side of the road. Every pose seemed alien and timeless. There were animals all over the place: goats, dogs, chickens, and cattle, all part of the Arusha scene.

When we left Arusha, we really left. What roads! They build

Warusha woman planting crops.
Previous page: Young Warusha tribesmen.

paved roads, usually with foreign aid, but when the rains come the earth base is washed away, creating huge potholes. Maintaining the roads is an expensive proposition, and after a while everyone gives up and the potholes remain, so there are sometimes roads full of great cavities, going nowhere. It was easier to drive on the side, off the tarmac, but it was still very bumpy and extremely dusty.

The dust was everywhere. In my nose, in my eyes, in my clothes. I was dirty right away. It was difficult breathing, too, and I began coughing away like mad. I suddenly understood why cowboys tied neckerchiefs around their necks. It was not just for glamour. I got out a neckerchief and tied it around my nose, stuffing the lower fold into my mouth. This eliminated a good deal of the dust problem and helped breathing, particularly through my mouth. It took me a while to work out a system, perhaps half a day, and it took me another full day to work the dust out of my lungs. But by then I didn't care.

We travelled through miles of flat, open country. A geography lesson. It was much hotter than I expected, and I drank constantly from my portable water bottle.

Already, as I took in the wide open expanse of Africa, sparse and bare in practically every direction, Canada and North America seemed millions of miles away. I was in seventh heaven. I didn't want to talk. I was driving farther and farther away from the financial world of Bay Street.

The landscape was warm and brown. Hot brown, deep brown, brown brown. There was dust everywhere, on everything: on the animals, the birds, on the brown water. I kept looking at the little pools beside the road and saying to myself bilharzia, bilharzia. Long before getting to Africa I had read about and been warned about these trematodes, flukes that carry bilharziasis or schistosomiasis. These almost invisible parasites are picked up when one goes wading or swimming in stagnant pools, contaminated lakes, and some rivers. The dangerous disease affects the organs above the pelvic area. It is extremely difficult to cure and requires a long recovery period.

It got hotter and drier as we descended the rocky road into the Rift Valley. This was rough driving at its worst, and we could only travel slowly. It was almost too hot to have lunch.

Halfway through the day, with the going still slow and rough, we drew near to the dramatic clouded cone of Oldonyo Lengai, home of the great god Lengai, according to Maasai legend. The

The clouded summit of Oldonyo Lengai, home of the great god Lengai, and the only active volcano in Africa.

only remaining active volcano in Africa, it dominates a landscape covered by volcanic lava and silt and black dust. It last erupted in 1967, spewing fine grey ash over its barren kingdom.

> *The Maasai say that Lengai or Ngai moved to this place in the sky after a Dorobo hunter shot an arrow at him, and most of the day for most of the year his realm is hidden; now Ngai is remote, beyond their reach, and they are visited by death and famine.*
>
> **PETER MATTHIESSEN The Tree Where Man Was Born**

Still we descended, along the eastern valley below the Rift Valley Escarpment, heading towards the south end of Lake Natron. This is Maasai country, with a few trees and some signs of civilization in the form of occasional semi-circles of mud huts and small herds of cattle grazing, though on what I couldn't imagine, for there was little grass.

Our first sight of African game, a small herd of zebra some distance away, was unspectacular. However, our first sight of giraffes was truly thrilling. These wonderfully tall angular beasts, forever trimming the tops of thorn bushes, never stopped fascinating me. They were as curious about us as we were about them, and their long slender necks and small heads silhouetted against the clear blue African sky remains one of the most characteristic sights of East Africa. The ancient Egyptians thought the giraffe to be the unlikely result of a mating between a leopard and a camel.

> *The tallest animal in the world had stirred the imagination of man from the earliest times. It was painted on rocks by the bushmen, immortalized on tomb walls by ancient Egyptians, and paraded by the Romans. For the Arabs it played an important role in maintaining stability in Middle Eastern politics. The rarity, gentleness, and beauty of the giraffe made it a perfect gift as a token of goodwill and peace.*
>
> **CYNTHIA MOSS Portraits in the Wild**

Later in the afternoon we also had our first sight of ostriches. They are skittish, unkempt-looking great birds, and instantly brought to mind Bernhard Grzimek's observations in *Serengeti Shall Not Die*:

> *An ostrich cock in love behaves just as oddly as a man in the same predicament. The ostrich sits on his long legs and rhythmically beats his wings alternately on either side. He puts his head back and rubs the nape of his neck along his back. His neck and legs are a shining red colour at this time. To us this may seem a strange way for the largest living bird to behave but the hens know its meaning. They run away playfully, and he chases after them with giant strides.*

The males are darker than the females, and the difference is a form of camouflage, for the males sit on the eggs at night, while the lighter-coloured females sit on them by day.

We dropped altitude for about an hour, driving down towards Lake Natron. The scrub thickened and a few thorn trees appeared. We were very tired — tired of driving and being bumped around and being hot and dehydrated. We were looking forward to some kind of cover or shade. But you could not take away the excitement.

Waiting for us at the campsite were Joshua Mbowe and Richard Laizier. They were the advance camp and had set up the small tan nylon tents in a dusty open clearing near a narrow river. Again I immediately thought, bilharzia. Be careful. But we swam in it anyway. We were too hot and desperate to cool off to care very much. That is the real danger.

What a place for a camp. It was not at all what I had expected. There were some tall thorn bushes around, some scrub, and the odd tree. It was dirty and hot and in the middle of nowhere. The Maasai were close, perhaps a quarter of a mile away.

The tents were very low and again not quite what I had expected. Thad had forgotten his tent, but he was not in the least concerned. He bunked in with Joshua and Richard in the smallest tent — though sharing a very close confined space is not the most comfortable existence when it is that hot. Inside the tents were little low cots, sleeping bags, and a single blanket, which we certainly did not

Thad Petersen, a versatile safari leader, is totally relaxed in the African bush.

need. Mosquitoes at night were bad. But it was exhilarating none the less. There was no world other than the present.

> *There is a popular misconception that Swahili is the language spoken throughout the African continent. In fact, Swahili is spoken primarily in Kenya and Tanzania and to a lesser degree as far west as eastern Zaire .... There are several hundred distinct African languages that make their speakers unintelligible to one another. For this reason at independence most African countries adopted the language of their former colonizer as their national language. A few countries have changed their policy and adopted a major African language, making the European language a second language. However, in today's technological world this places such countries at an economic disadvantage. Inevitably foreign words must be incorporated into the African language, adulterating the purity of that language.*
>
> Jane and Leah Taylor **Fielding's Literary Africa**

Richard Laizier and Joshua Mbowe — the advance camp.

Joshua and Richard and Thad were happy, friendly, and attentive, and I felt very much at ease with all of them. I found out that Joshua lives at the foot of Kilimanjaro and is from the Chagga tribe. The three of them were on very good terms and talked much of the time in Swahili. Thad spoke only Swahili to Joshua and Richard.

Both Joshua and Richard at one time would have been called bearers, although I hate that term. Thad called them the advance camp. With the tents in the back of the truck they go ahead to set up camp. They do all the cooking and construct the makeshift outhouse as well as an ingenious outdoor shower — a great luxury. They are nice, easy-going people and comfortable to talk to. They seem to laugh a lot when they are by themselves.

Thad Petersen loves the outdoor life. He loves camping, being out in the wild, sitting around the campfire with a billycan, or simply sitting on top of his Land Rover looking at the world through his binoculars. It is impossible not to like him. He is a natural leader and exudes that knowledgeable confidence that makes everyone in his charge at ease. He is thirty-three years old, and went to high school in Kenya, to university in the United States, and after that got back to outdoor life in Tanzania as soon as he possibly could.

Exhausted by the day's drive and the shock of being catapulted

Although the ostrich's wings are useless for flying, they are used for braking and turning. They also provide shade for chicks and are useful for swishing away flies. The ostrich has extremely keen eyesight, and when running from a predator can reach speeds of up to fifty miles an hour.

in a day and a half into the middle of Africa, I piled into my tent determined to have a good night's sleep. But it was impossible to get to sleep.

I loved Ceylon, where I was born. My childhood there was idyllic. For generations our family had been tea planters, wealthy and socially prominent. They and their friends were exuberant, confident people who lived life fully. As a child I looked forward to doing the same.

We lived mostly on our tea estate and I grew up out of doors. It was a birdwatcher's paradise, and I still remember many of the hundreds of species that we could see. I was serious about birds and when I was young made a comprehensive and valuable collection of birds' eggs.

All wilderness in Ceylon is called jungle, including the semi-arid thorn-brush country and mangroves of the coastal areas, the marshy, mosquito-infested glades of the Mahaweli Basin, the dry hills of Kantali, and the fern-filled dripping rain forests of the hill country. Most of the wildlife of the island is concentrated in the national parks. One that we visited from time to time, Ruhuna, more commonly known as Yala, is tucked away in the south-eastern corner of the island. It is a semi-arid area, mainly thorny scrub forest. Whenever I could convince my father, he would take us, and sometimes me alone, to this dry paradise. The landscape was very like the Africa I was now experiencing.

Sometimes we would stay in the Hambantota rest house, or better still in one of the little bungalows available inside the park, if we could get one. These had few modern comforts. At night, light was provided by oil lamps, and I still associate the pungent smell of burning kerosene with those early years. We were surrounded by the sound of the jungle. The bungalows were close to a jungle tank and water hole, and large herds of deer, wild boar, and even elephants wandered past. I can still remember the deer — sambur, barking deer, musk deer, spotted deer — all of them. Outside the park we used to hunt them, not for trophies but for the pot. Once on our way home from Yala I shot one of these beautiful creatures with my twelve-bore. It was the last time I shot anything.

At the little bungalow one of the guides would cook simple meals of rice and vegetable curry for us. These guides, or trackers as we called them, were marvellously accommodating and friendly people, and it was they who introduced me to the wonders of the jungle and instilled in me a love of nature. Here my father and I would spend time together talking about absolutely anything and everything that came into our heads.

All this life was swept away when I was thirteen. I went to school in England, my parents separated, we lost much of our family property, and the rest was nationalized by the new independent Ceylon government. I never saw my father again and I never went back to Ceylon. But lying here remembering, in a setting much like that of an earlier time, I felt that that idyllic life was not so distant after all.

Waterbucks are more relaxed and less frightened of predators than other antelopes, as carnivores seem repelled by the strong musky smell given off by their skin glands. This female Defassa waterbuck's coarse shaggy coat is a further impediment to threatening killers.

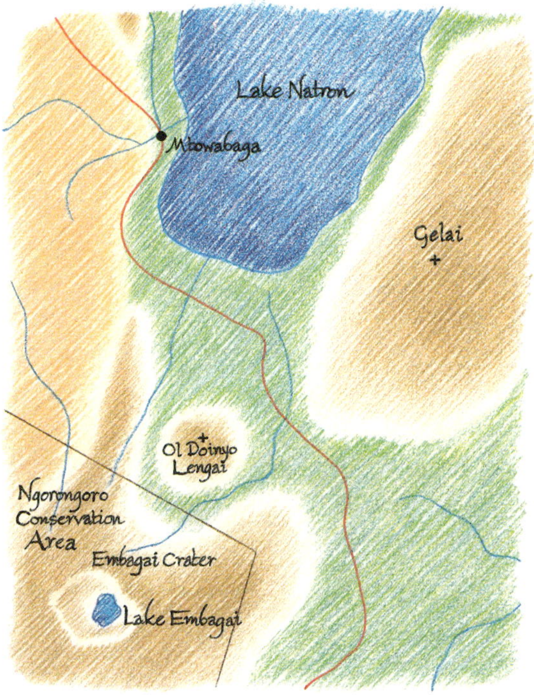

CHAPTER THREE

The Second Day

Dawn broke slowly, pale green and shewed a landscape which looked like scientific places of the moon, a wilderness of broken rocky hills, as green and bare as brittle glass. Then the sun came up and the hills were brown, rusty, barren, not at all like any romantic idea of Africa, but much better of course, because they are real.

JOYCE CARY **Railway Camp**

In the morning it was still hot. I could hear Joshua and Richard talking quietly and I could hear the fire crackling and the clatter of tin plates. It was semi-dark.

The water in the canvas tripod was warm without having to be heated. I shaved with my electric razor, which still had a remnant of charge. I then washed, spitting into the dusty earth while brushing my teeth, noticing this white thing, toothpaste, incongruous in the dusty earth, and then covering it up with my boot. The water droplets bounced up dust. I put on a clean pair of shorts and a clean shirt — still fashion conscious.

I also made my first inspection of the safari outhouse — a deep hole, a home-made seat with pegs for legs, and a green wraparound tarpaulin for privacy.

Joshua had brewed a pot of Tanzanian coffee by throwing a net bag of coarsely ground beans into a pot of boiling water. It was thick, filled with grounds, strong and bitter, and needed to be well spliced with sugar.

As we were finishing breakfast we were visited by four bare-headed Maasai women, the three younger ones each with a child strapped to her back. They must have come from their *boma,* or encampment, about a quarter of a mile away. There wasn't much conversation. They merely sat around the edge of the camp and watched us with polite curiosity, while one of them breast-fed her child.

> *Native women shave their heads, and it is a curious thing how quickly you yourself will come to feel that these little round neat skulls, which look like some kind of dusky nuts, are the sign of true womanliness, and that a crop of hair on the head of a woman is as unladylike as a beard.*
>
> Isak Dinesen **Out of Africa**

The plan was to spend the morning hiking up the Ngera Sera River towards its source near the edge of the Rift Valley Escarpment. Well supplied with water and insect repellent, we walked first across the grazing grounds of the Maasai herdsmen — dry, rocky fields that still seemed to have a few shoots of grass for the cattle — then up along the banks of the river that flowed shallow and muddy over a bed of fine volcanic silt.

We began to climb. With shoes and socks still on, we waded back and forth across the river, which grew narrower and faster as we approached its source. We crossed and recrossed it many times, scrambling over the rocks and black sand. The vegetation changed and the temperature cooled as we climbed to the higher altitude. Eventually we came to two waterfalls of spectacular beauty and walked into a dark, cool cavern under the first to get to the second. We were surrounded by palm trees and other tropical flora, all unfamiliar. There was a smell of baboon dung, although we didn't see any baboons.

We cooled off and continued our climb. Our route took us up precipitous rock faces with only the most rudimentary hand and foot grips to save us from falling. There were two climbs above the falls where a single false step would have caused death or at least serious injury. Arriving in mid-morning high up on the valley wall, we came upon four streams of water gushing out of the cliff face. This was the source of the river. Above the crest of the Rift Valley the vultures soared in ever-increasing circles.

Just after 1:00 p.m. we returned to camp for lunch after a very hazardous and circuitous journey along the narrow mountain path that ran only four or five feet from the high edge of the valley's sheer face. There were landslides across the little track in several places, and although we had actually taken the path to avoid descending the two dangerous rock faces, I found this longer journey much more terrifying. Thad, thank God, had the sure feet of a mountain goat and I followed his heels with my eyes the whole way.

After a few hours spent sweltering motionless in the afternoon heat and swapping tales, I found the blisters on my feet from the morning climb so painful that I had to do something about them. Most could be mended fairly easily with the application of Band-Aids, but fine black sand had made its way through the punctured skin of my right large toe and it made walking very painful. Joshua volunteered to fix it. With serious intent he extracted a razor blade from his small travelling bag and proceeded with a steady hand to cut all the way around the perimeter of the large blister on the sole of the toe. With one sure clean circular incision he removed the outlying skin. Then with two or three hard jets of air which he propelled from his mouth he blew the irritating black sand out of the sensitive wound. He then covered the base of my toe with some mysterious dark grey grease. The whole procedure was painless and quick.

Joshua warned me not to walk around barefoot in Africa as I might pick up small parasites called chigoes, which penetrate the human skin to lay eggs. He said he had got the expertise to deal with my blister from attending to chigoes that had established themselves in the toes of his fellow tribesmen. Once a chigoe has worked its way into your skin — and it is impossible to see — it causes a considerable amount of itching, which will continue and become increasingly unpleasant until the chigoe is removed. Removing the chigoe requires a great deal of skill because the sack that it creates under your skin, and into which the eggs are laid, must be totally removed without breaking. Otherwise, the eggs will penetrate other parts of the flesh. All Africans are taught to deal with this nasty business, and they become adept at removing the uncomfortable parasite with a razor blade or sharp knife and a pin

The remains of a African buffalo in the mud flats near Lake Natron. Its horns closely resemble those on a Viking's helmet.

or needle. Joshua explained that removing chigoes from fellow Africans' feet is a definite tribal responsibility.

In the afternoon we set off for Lake Natron. The journey over dry, flat plains and baked mud pans was extraordinarily hot. For some time Thad had been looking for a mythically large crocodile in one of the pools off the main lake, and so we too looked, driving and walking, but mainly just walking around a terrain that must be very similar to a moonscape. Over completely barren and arid land, we walked miles to get to the water. When we eventually did get near, the ground underfoot became very slippery. There was obviously water just beneath the surface. It was dangerously boggy; if you stopped, you settled and sank. We could see the remains of animals and birds that had been trapped and had perished in the mud.

In the distance on the lake we could see flamingoes. But before we made the journey to the lake, we spent a good part of the afternoon going around small lagoons and flats, investigating the seemingly lifeless pools. We drove and walked for miles over the flat dry wilderness. Birds and sand and mud.

One day Denys and I flew to Lake Natron... the place from where they take soda. The bottom of the lake and the shores are like some sort of whitish concrete, with a strong, sour and salt smell.

The sky was blue, but as we flew from the plains in over the stony and bare lower country, all colour seemed to be scorched out of it.... Here live thousands of Flamingoes, although I do not know how they exist in the brackish water — surely there are no fish here. At our approach they spread out in large circles and fans, like the rays of a setting sun, like an artful Chinese pattern on silk or porcelain, forming itself and changing, as we looked at it.

ISAK DINESEN **Out of Africa**

Back in the Jeep we first returned to where the zebra herds were and then drove out to Lake Natron, where we had to walk out at least half a mile. Mud again. It was disappointing because we couldn't get close enough to the flamingoes. I had to be satisfied with simple pink silhouettes. It was frustrating to see more through my binoculars than with my Leica, one of the two cameras I had with me, even though I got out the tripod and used a 500 mm telescopic lens.

Lake Natron is huge — thirty-five miles long and fifteen miles wide. To the naked eye it looks even bigger because of the wide flat regions surrounding it.

The nauseating smell of soda in the hot dry afternoon came from saline mineral deposits, which lie at the edge of the murky water. In the distance flamingoes embroidered the water's edge, a pink ribbon, dense, undulating, occasionally breaking apart and rising in flight. I longed to be engulfed in the pink cloud.

The flocks of flamingoes mirrored in the silent, still, and lonely lake made a thin line across most of the lake's southern tip. Through my binoculars I could see the two different species: the lesser with its dark red bill and the greater with a light pink bill that is black at the end. As we got closer the birds kept moving away until eventually, nervous of our constant approach, they stretched their necks and flew off in a beautiful crescent formation — a whole movement of pink blurring the sky — until they eventually settled to our right and introduced a new band of colour to that otherwise dull and lifeless corner of the lake.

Driving over sand dunes, black silt sand, and dry parched soda flats, we explored the smugglers' track between Tanzania and Kenya. The road is not marked on any map, and smugglers can use it to cross the Tanzania-Kenya border undetected. A desolate track in a desolate country, it is littered with bones of fallen wildebeest, and offers only infrequent sightings of zebra and oryx. It was silent, except for the occasional isolated cry of some bird. And always, not far away, the looming presence of Oldonyo Lengai and the great god Lengai looking down from his kingdom on everything and everyone in the arid Rift Valley plain.

At dusk we returned to camp, stopping now and then to watch baboons, ostriches, small herds of wildebeest and zebra, and a family of Maasai giraffe. (The common giraffe, Tanzania's most numerous giraffe, is called the Maasai giraffe because most of the Serengeti is Maasai territory.) The morning climb, the heat of the afternoon, the impact of all that we had seen, had exhausted us. Thad and I had two strong glasses of Sundowner gin with tonic before dinner. It practically blew our heads off. The locally brewed

Every zebra is different — each has a characteristically individual marking as personal and unique as a human fingerprint.

or distilled gin was bottled by Mahonda Liquors in Zanzibar, under Zanzibar government supervision, which wasn't much consolation.

As we sat around the campfire before our dinner of bananas and eland stew, Thad told us this story of how the zebra got his stripes:

In the old days, a very long time ago, all the animals were white. And they lived together in perfect harmony on the great open plains. Then the great god directed all the animals to a huge open cave that contained all the new clothes that the animals were going to wear. Each animal could choose his own clothes, and also his own headgear.

The leopard chose his beautiful coat, as did the cheetah. They were the earliest to arrive and chose first. The lion selected his golden mantle and his enormous mane which he put around his neck. The kudu chose his great spiral horns and the bongo his unique striped coat, and so on and so on. But the zebra, taking his time because he had found an unusually lush piece of grass, kept on eating.

The animals kept lining up and choosing from the many assorted outfits and headpieces. The sable antelope picked his spectacular scimitar-shaped horns, the topi his rich brown coat with black leggings, the rhinoceros his horn, the elephant his trunk, and so on and so on. But still the zebra took his time. He found another lush piece of grass, and kept on eating.

Finally, after all the animals had made their choices, the zebra, who was now very full, in fact quite over-stuffed, trotted slowly to the cave where all that was left was a very small black overcoat. It didn't fit him — particularly in his current rotund state — but there was nothing else, so he put it on. It took a long time because it was very small, but he stretched and stretched, and he pulled and pulled, and he wiggled and waggled, until finally and inevitably the coat split in several places, showing the zebra's true whiteness underneath.

And that was how the zebra got his stripes.

Zebras are dependent on water and seldom stray far from a water hole. Although the black and white stripes are conspicuous during the day, at dawn and at dusk, when most predators hunt, the stripes seem to blend together and zebras become harder to see.

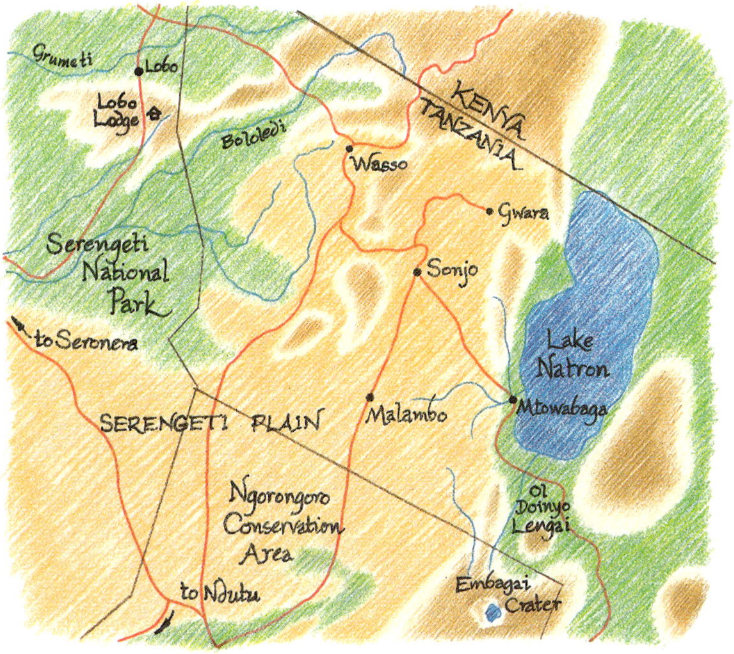

CHAPTER FOUR

Serengeti

Perhaps it is because there is more sky in Africa than anywhere else that one is constantly aware of the curious and exotic silhouettes of the trees, whether isolated on the stretching plain or looming in the early morning mists from the rain forests on the mountain sides.

ILKA CHASE **Elephants Arrive at Half-Past Five**

The immensity of the Rift Valley is staggering. It is a geological phenomenon, a monumental fracture in the earth's surface, stretching four thousand miles from the Jordan Valley in Israel, across the Red Sea into Ethiopia, and then down through Kenya and Tanzania into Mozambique where it finally reaches the sea again. It is literally splitting Africa into two, and millions of years hence the whole area east of the Rift Valley will have pulled away to form a separate continent.

The drive from our campsite up the great Rift Valley Escarpment and then along the top of the escarpment to Wasso on the western side of Lake Natron was truly spectacular. Once we were at the top, the Rift Valley lay naked and exposed, fifteen hundred feet below us, its edges sheer and sharp. Now that we were away from the hot lower plains around Lake Natron, the higher lands around us took on a much more colourful hue with violently contrasting bands of red, brown, and green, all exaggerated by the blinding sun.

First crossing the almost dried-out Monik River, we made our way up the new stony track to the rim of the Rift Valley. Then, with spectacular views of the valley, we wound along the rim, through Maasai lands across the Salei Plains, north and west to the lands of the Sonjo.

The Sonjo are a small tribe who have had to fight hard to protect their territory from the Maasai. Their relatively small area of land is right in the corner of the Maasai lands, and here they farm and breed goats and cattle, with some government help. The Sonjo

Sonjo children still play with bows and arrows on the western slopes of the Rift Valley. The Sonjo continue to fight and argue determinedly with the Maasai over their bordering lands.

Previous page: Wildebeest in the evening light.

A pair of nesting white-backed vultures silhouetted against the afternoon sun scan the plains for carrion.

are a poor people but retain many of their ancient traditions, like scarring the women on their high cheekbones and under the left breast. They still protect their territory with bows and poison-tipped arrows. The Sonjo villages, not more than half a dozen, are spread along the western slopes of the Rift Valley and all overlook Oldonyo Lengai. They too, like the Maasai, believe Oldonyo Lengai to be the mountain of god.

From Wasso we headed west towards the boundary of the Serengeti National Park. It is the largest park in Tanzania and one of the largest wildlife sanctuaries in the world — 5,700 square miles in area. The park lies on a high plateau between the Ngorongoro Highlands and the Kenya-Tanzania border and extends almost to Lake Victoria.

The Serengetti Plains... are the great sanctuary of the Maasai People and they harbour more wild game than any similar territory in all of East Africa. In the season of drought they are as dry and tawny as the coats of the lion that prowl them, and during the rains they provide the benison of soft grass to all the animals in a child's picture book.

They are endless and they are empty, but they are as warm with life as the waters of a tropic sea. They are webbed with the paths of eland and wildebeest and Thompson's gazelle and their hollows and valleys are trampled by thousands of zebra. I have seen a herd of buffalo invade the pastures under the occasional thorn tree groves and, now and then, the whimsically fashioned figure of a plodding rhino has moved along the horizon like a grey boulder come to life....

Beryl Markham **West with the Night**

What Beryl Markham wrote about the Serengeti in *West with the Night* is as true today as it was half a century ago, except that the rhinos are now seldom seen in the plains. As we drove through the north-eastern part of the park we saw an incredible amount of game. Oryx, dik-diks, ostriches, Grant's gazelle, Thomson's gazelle, wildebeest, hartebeest, impala, topi, antelope, and a pair of very aggressive African buffalo. A pair of white-backed vultures made a fine picture silhouetted on a dead branch against the afternoon sun, and I caught a glimpse of a smiling bat-eared fox outside her den.

The park's name, Serengeti, comes from the Maasai language and means "endless plains". The park encompasses the main part of the Serengeti eco-system and, as in all eco-systems, the vegetation and types of animals you find are closely correlated. The park's principal geographical areas are the short- and long-grass open plains in the south-east, the acacia savannah in the central area, the hilly, more densely wooded northern section, and the extensive woodland and black clay plains dominated by the central ranges of mountain in the western corridor. Associated with these zones are different types of animals. Giraffes, for example, need trees to browse and so will not be found in the open plains. Lions, on the other hand, follow the migrating wildebeest and are therefore found on the open plains.

The migrating animals, in particular the wildebeest and some gazelles and zebra, graze in the south-eastern plains during the wet season from December until May and then move west into the woodlands, later spreading north into the Maasai Mara. With the end of the dry season in November, they return to the plains.

Despite the constant threat of poaching, the Serengeti is a success story. The wildebeest herd increased from 250,000 in 1960 to over 1.5 million in the early 1980s and has kept fairly stable since then. Zebras have maintained a population of about 200,000 since 1960, probably kept so by lions and other predators. Lions are hard to count accurately, but they breed rapidly, and specialists believe that they too are increasing and may number around 3,000. Elephants have moved into the Serengeti in the last thirty years, pushed out of other areas by increasing human activity and poaching. Today the Serengeti has about 2,000, but even here they are under constant threat from ivory poachers.

A small, nervous animal with huge ears, the bat-eared fox seldom moves far from its den, feeding on any small rodents and insects, as well as scorpions, that it can find in its restricted territory.

The animal that is most endangered by poaching is the rhinoceros. In the early 1970s the park contained about five hundred black rhinos. Today fewer than twenty survive. The animal is slaughtered for its horn, which is not a true horn, but made of hard-packed hair and keratin.

> *The rhino is a remarkable animal in that copulation lasts for quite a long time compared to the few seconds most animals take. Rhino copulate for thirty minutes or even longer... (and) the lengthy copulation might be one reason behind the belief that the rhino's horn is an aphrodisiac. The shape of the horn is considered phallic and must also be an important element behind the myth.*
>
> CYNTHIA MOSS **Portraits in the Wild**

Just before I left for Africa, thirty heavily armed poachers had slaughtered five white rhinos in Kenya's Meru National Park and had traded gunfire with wardens before escaping. The temptation to poach is great: prized in Asia as an aphrodisiac and in Yemen for making dagger handles, a single rhino horn can fetch as much as $24,000. In Kenya black rhinos have been reduced in number from 20,000 in 1970 to only 450 today.

Hunting is prohibited within the Serengeti park, but killing occurs none the less. As Dr Markus Borner, the Frankfurt Zoological Society's representative in the park, points out, some animals are killed by local hunters to provide themselves and their families with food. This time-honoured practice of hunting to meet local needs does not seriously threaten the animal populations. Recently, however, highly organized teams of professional hunters have begun to operate in the park in response to an expanding market for such things as wildebeest meat. Tanzania's national anti-poaching unit, established in 1978 to combat this new menace, lacks the resources needed to mount a truly effective counter-attack over the vast area of the park.

As we reached Lobo at the north end of the Serengeti a line of

The adult black rhino has no natural enemies except man. It is so near-sighted as to be virtually blind, and its precious horns impair its vision even more. Today there are probably fewer than twenty black rhinos left in Tanzania.

As we approached Lobo at the north end of the Serengeti, we saw a pair of crowned cranes performing their intricate mating dance.

wildebeest crossed the road, while nearby a small herd of zebra and three giraffes munched on their late-afternoon meal. Near the road a pair of crowned cranes put on a dancing display for us.

Lobo Lodge is set high on a massive outcrop of rock with a panoramic view of the Serengeti Plains. The lodge is boldly designed and built into the faults and contours of a rock, called a kopje. Kopjes are a characteristic of the plains. Animals — lions, cheetahs, wild dogs — take cover in them or climb up onto them for a lookout point.

On the kopjes were many rock hyraxes, small rodent-like animals. At first I thought they gave off a strange odour but later discovered that an indigenous plant was responsible for the nasty,

Large, stately, and essentially terrestrial birds, crowned cranes have a loud, elongated honking call often likened to that of the Canada goose.

dung-like smell. Surprisingly, hyraxes are the closest known relative to the elephant.

Troops of olive baboons bounding around gave us a glimpse of the strict discipline and order maintained by a powerful elite or clique of adult males who are constantly concerned with their position in the troop. Status is everything for a baboon.

We arrived at Lobo late in the afternoon, but I persuaded Thad to continue driving, while there was still daylight, down to the arid river valleys in the hope of spotting a leopard. I was developing leopard fever — partly, I suppose, because of the challenge and mystery represented by this most elusive of cats.

Notes on leopards: A leopard is the only known animal other than man that will kill for the sake of killing. African lore is full of stories of the nocturnal habits of this beautiful cat that has often been reported to steal and eat villagers' children. It is smaller than a lion but can tear its prey apart with its hind legs while its sharp jaws lock into its victim's throat to strangle it. It is fierce and extremely dangerous when cornered. Joshua told a story of a well-known man-eater in the Musoma district that escaped the continued attack of twelve warriors with spears, managing to injure ten of them with its claws before making its getaway. This happened only a few years ago.

Leopards will eat any food, including predators and carrion. However, the animal's favourite foods include a wide range of birds and mammals, among them guinea fowl, spurfowl, wart hogs, hares, and particularly the smaller antelopes like the impala, reedbuck, waterbuck, and gazelle. Leopards are also particularly partial to monkeys and baboons, as well as domestic stock like sheep, goats, and calves, and domestic dogs.

They are large cats, powerfully built, but vary considerably in size and weight. A large leopard can weigh as much as two hundred pounds, but an average weight for the animal is one hundred and ten pounds. They stand about thirty inches high at the shoulder. The full length of a leopard, including its tail, can reach up to five feet.

There is no mistaking its colour. Its soft short fur with numerous "rosettes" on a creamy yellow or yellowish-grey background is spectacularly beautiful. At a distance the darker colours tend to merge, producing a grey effect, but the underside of the animal, including its chin, throat, breast, stomach, and the inside upper part of its sturdy legs, is almost pure white. Its tail is long, spotted, and has a black tip.

Leopards are territorial animals and their range varies very much according to food supply. A leopard's territory can be as little as one-half square mile and as much as four square miles. Leopards mark their areas by calling with their hoarse saw-like cough or by spraying their urine on trees, branches, bushes, anthills, rocks, and any other prominent landscape feature. With their sharp claws they also mark trees, rocks, and places on the ground.

The leopard's voice is barely audible. Its rasping cough is used not only as a territorial claim but also as a form of greeting or con-

Impalas are gregarious animals. Male impalas sometimes collect herds of anywhere from twenty to a hundred females of which they are most protective. Males fight often, especially during the rutting season, and it is difficult for a male to keep his position of power with his female herd for very long. After a month or two he is usually ousted and, ironically, has to join the bachelor herd from which his adversary has come.

tact. Alarm or anger transforms the cough into a deeper growl that becomes at times a screaming roar. A leopard's contented purr is sometimes more audible than its cough.

The stealthiest of hunters, leopards are almost impossible to see at night except with luck and in the headlights of a Jeep or Land Rover. Thad had never seen one at night. During the day they hide in the long thick grass or in the clefts in kopjes or caves.

The leopard is a solitary and secretive inhabitant of thickets, an animal of darkness. These characteristics have been both its salvation and its doom. By remaining out of sight it has been able to survive near dense human habitation, areas from which other large cats have long vanished. But whereas the lion invokes goodwill by displaying its indolent, seemingly carefree nature, the leopard conveys visions of a nocturnal marauder, of a cold, detached personality. Friendliness leads to friendliness. By virtue of its being so withdrawn, the leopard has received little sympathy from man and now desperately needs it. Persecuted for its lovely hide, it maintains only a precarious foothold where it was formerly abundant. Every woman who needs to satisfy her vanity with a leopard-skin coat should first contemplate the exquisite beauty of this cat in repose.

GEORGE B. SCHALLER Serengeti: A Kingdom of Predators

A creature unique and paradoxical, sinister and ruthless, the leopard is at the same time charismatic and vulnerable.

In our two hours of exploring the lowlands we saw no leopard. In fact we hadn't yet seen any of the African cats. We returned to the lodge to take advantage of the shower facilities and then went in to dinner. I remember thinking then that I would far rather tent than stay in a lodge which took away the sense of freedom. Even though I was car-weary after the long day of driving, I realized that I was getting acclimatized to Africa. I understood now the simple fact that khaki is worn because it doesn't show the dirt. What I wore and what I ate were becoming less and less important.

It is almost impossible to believe the zoologists' claim, based on anatomical similarities, that the rock hyrax is the closest living relative of the elephant! They frequent the kopjes, living in colonies within a very circumscribed home range.

CHAPTER FIVE

The Fourth Day

In the dry season, the sun scorched the harsh grass to a dry biscuit colour and you could see heat shimmering over the ridges ahead. Doves cooed tirelessly from their branches, yellow weaver birds chattered, and sometimes you could see a bustard, good for the pot, strutting through the grass.

NELLIE GRANT **Nellie: Letters From Africa**

I almost felt that I'd earned the Serengeti. We had already accomplished quite a lot. We'd driven right across Tanzania from Arusha to Lake Natron and had experienced a couple of very hot nights with dust, flies, and discomfort. But we still hadn't seen anything fantastic. So, rising very early in the morning we set off for Seronera. Right off the bat, we encountered a troop of baboons. Hundreds of them. And then, only a little way from the lodge, on a rough dirt road descending into the Serengeti, there he was.

I saw him through the long brown grass, almost totally camouflaged, looking up at me with his head no higher than the grass. The instant our eyes met he sank down. I said almost in a whisper, "There's a lion!" Thad stopped the Land Rover, but all you could see was the grass. And I said, "There." You could just see the top of the tawny head, which would alternately raise itself a little and then sink out of view again.

The lion, an enormous male, walked away slowly and silently through the grass. We turned the Land Rover around to get a little closer to him. Suddenly there was a terrible smell. Thad said, "One thing about lions, lion dung makes an awful, awful smell." Obviously the lion had just defecated by the side of the road and had gone on. I wanted to get out and onto higher land by the side of the Land Rover to get a decent photograph. But Thad said, "I don't think you'd better, because that might not be our lion's dung." And just as I said, "What do you mean?" I had the answer to my question.

A lion's roar can be heard from as far as six miles away. It is the most thrilling and unsettling sound of the African wilderness. The call, usually made up of a series of climaxing grunts, is heard in the late evening and before sunrise.

Previous page: Wet cheetah, hunting.

Another male lion moved to within twenty yards of where we were. It was *his* dung we had smelled. Slowly he turned, looked at us, and moved off towards the other lion.

This was certainly a close view. Closer than we had expected. Later on we saw many lions, but as Thad said, "You know, those two were really wild, and were probably hunting. You don't see many like that so close. I think we surprised them."

Seeing your first lion is a thrill. There is a sense of fear in your bones. Our experience with the lions gave us a good basic lesson of how dangerous it is to leave the safety of your Land Rover. You never know, whether on a kopje or under a tree, what is around. Even on a road anything can happen and happen fast.

On the other hand, man need have no fear of a cheetah, a nervous animal. Sighting a cheetah is a stirring experience, too. Minutes after the lions disappeared from view we spotted the silhouettes of two cheetahs on a kopje a couple of hundred yards away.

I used the 300 mm lens on my Canon EOS 650 to track the two cheetahs, probably two young males, also on a morning hunt. When they saw us they moved farther away. Cheetahs are atypical of the cats. They are built for speed rather than power. With their trim waists and long slender legs, their deep chests and small heads, there is majesty and grace in their haughty, lazy movements. A faint tilt of a head, a switch of a tail in counterpoint to the waving grass, emphasizes their disdainful attitude to the world in general and us in particular.

Cheetahs actually are quite plentiful in the park but are more easily observed in the plains. Sometimes mistaken for a leopard, the cheetah is taller and more lightly built with rounded spots dotted over its body and dark "tear" marks that almost join the corners of the eyes to the mouth. It is wonderfully long and graceful with an ill-defined short mane on its hind neck and shoulders. The cheetah is remarkable among the cats in not being able to retract its claws. Female cheetahs are always solitary, but males sometimes form groups of two or three. So the two cheetahs that we saw that morning were almost certainly two young males.

The long, slender cheetah is different from the leopard in that its coat is covered with round black dots rather than grouped rosettes. Its athletic legs and small, drooping head are two other characteristic features. Although cheetahs tend to be migratory in the Serengeti, there is some proof that they are also territorial. They leave their scent by spraying urine on trees, rocks, and other landmarks.

That morning drive to Seronera continued to be an astonishing feast of wildlife viewing — thousands of wildebeest, topi, hartebeest, giraffe, and a close study of a drooling female hyena on her way back to her cubs after a night on the prowl. We also had our first look at waterbucks and glimpsed briefly a crocodile in the Seronera River. A slow-moving, solitary leopard tortoise allowed us a close inspection. Families of wart hogs hustled away, keeping their distance.

> *The thing about "wart-piggies" is that they don't have to do anything to be funny except just being there. Their disproportionately huge, ugly heads, the ragged mane of coarse hair on the shoulder hump, the white "mutton chop" sideburns combined with dainty, little feet make one think of the outlandishly dressed "top bananas" of the burlesque of earlier days. But it is when he runs that the Wart Hog becomes a real wag. He trots off with rapid little mincing steps, albeit pitter-pattering as lightly as a cat, with his ridiculous, thin little tail stuck straight up like a tiny flag pole. His "flag" is a few stiff hairs that project horizontally from the tail tip. I always think of a slim-handled Japanese back-scratcher, the kind with the carved hand on the end.*
>
> TERENCE MICHAEL SHORTT **Not As the Crow Flies**

We reached the kopjes, said to be some of the oldest rocks on earth. These magnificent outcroppings, sometimes two or three billion years old, again showed another aspect of the grandeur of the African continent. Kopjes serve as host for a great variety of vegetation that one does not see on the plains. It is surprising to see the green of the island-like rock monuments against the burnt grasses of the savannah plains.

We stopped for lunch near one of these outcroppings and Thad said, "Go and see if there is anything dangerous around here." I crawled up the cracks of the kopje and took the camera off my neck and held it by its strap — my only defence. I was prepared to swing it if attacked. Thad usually checked every kopje if we stopped, but now I was doing it and wasn't very comfortable. I was also not checking very thoroughly because I wasn't at all anxious to find anything in the caves, where leopards or lions might be lurking away

Sounders of wart hogs are often seen in the Serengeti, particularly in the open savannahs. They have poor sight but their senses of smell and hearing are excellent. They often back into burrows in order to defend themselves with their unusually large tusks.

from the heat of the day. I had little enthusiasm for sighting a leopard under these conditions. I gave the caves a cursory glance. The only sign of wildlife was a solitary steinbok that bounded away. Even that small deer gave me a start.

Setting up the lunch meant putting down the back of the Land Rover. The tailgate became our table. Cheese, bread, sliced tomatoes, and cold coffee. Thad had a collapsible table that he sometimes put up, but I thought that far too pretentious and quite unnecessary.

Soon after lunch we stopped at Naabi, the headquarters and entrance to the Serengeti Game Reserve. We were on the lookout for

In the dry season, herds of up to a thousand African buffaloes may be seen — but never far from water.

African hunting dogs. I had heard and read much of the hunting skills of these notorious animals, now nearing extinction, and hoped to see their dens and pups. We spent more than an hour searching the plains with one of the Naabi guides before we saw a male hunting dog and knew that the den must be near. We were right and, although in the heat of the day the bitches and their pups were below ground, I was able to photograph one other male and two separate bitches in their dens. One of the bitches had a bloody muzzle, presumably from a successful morning hunt. Below ground we could hear the high-pitched yelps of the pups. These hunting dogs are a distinct species, further away in evolutionary terms from

domestic dogs than from wolves. They used to be seen in many parts of Africa but are now rare. They live and hunt in packs and have a complex and subtle social organization. The dogs usually make their kills early in the morning, between 6:00 a.m. and 8:00 a.m., and then again at night before dark.

Later on, a small pride of lions that included two males, two females, and two cubs offered some marvellous photographing opportunities, but my attention was somewhat distracted by my growing preoccupation with seeing a leopard. I had been told that there were three leopards in the Seronera River Valley — a female and two males — and as we passed through Seronera I could see that the small river valleys were ideal leopard country. Two narrow meandering rivers, bordered with the lusher bush and tree vegetation they encouraged, interrupted the grassy plains. Thorn acacias,

yellow fever-trees, and sausage trees flourished on the river banks, and bird and animal life was abundant. Reedbuck, Thomson's gazelle, and impala (favourite leopard food) were plentiful. With lots of shade trees and excellent cover for hunting, it was perfect for leopards. But still no luck.

Through the rest of the afternoon we drove past thousands of animals, particularly the various species of gazelles. All the time, I was being gently educated by Thad in how to distinguish, even at a distance, the different species. For example, Grant's and Thomson's gazelles look similar but the Grant's is larger and the Thomson's or "Tommy" constantly twitches its black tail across its white butt. The topi, with its rich deep rufous and black colouring and backward sloping horns, has a habit of putting its front legs onto a high part of an anthill to survey its territory and look out for predators. Then there is the ungainly silhouette of the wildebeest with its hunch-backed shoulders, lowered head and mane, and slender legs.

As we approached Lake Ndutu the scene had a magical quality. It was late in the afternoon, and a wonderful orange evening glow bathed the plains. We were making our way across the Serengeti towards our next campsite and looking forward to getting there. We were quite punchy and trading comments about what we would most like to see. A herd of elephants. A giraffe drinking. I wanted to see a kill...and a leopard. Also an African sunset. And I wanted to get a picture of wildebeest with the sun behind them and the evening light shining through their white beards.

The evening light in the Serengeti is extraordinary. Somehow the evening light didn't matter as much at Lake Natron or the Rift Valley. Even in the northern Serengeti, it was a pleasant light, but not magical as on that first evening at Lake Ndutu. I don't know why.

Lake Ndutu is spectacularly beautiful. There was an air of expectancy about it. Our campsite was near where Hugo van Lawick has his base. We could hear lions, see flamingoes. Under the spell of a perfect African evening even Thad wasn't saying a hell of a lot. On the way to the campsite we went right down to the northern effluence of the big lake and, I'm sure not by accident, we saw it all. Giraffes and zebra. Wildebeest crossing the shallow water. I can

As the African hunting dog peered out of her den, we heard behind her the high-pitched yelps of her pups. Among the most vicious of African predators, they hunt in packs and often consume their prey while still alive. They are very rarely seen alone or in small groups.

hear them now. A tripping, splashing sound. Giraffes skittish, wanting to drink, and then finally spreading their slender forelegs awkwardly, almost ashamedly, so that they could get their beautiful long necks down to the water.

There was a marvellous sense of harmony, of things coming together. Just as we were getting close to Lake Ndutu and approaching a secluded water hole quite near its northern tip, we saw a lioness lying patiently in the tall green grass on the edge of a small stream. She was waiting at the water hole for some prey to come by, looking for an early evening kill. Thad pointed her out very quietly. "There is a lioness there, just looking at us. Quite a way away." We could just see her ears through the green grass as she waited, observing everything, not moving at all, using the tall grass as cover. Ambush.

We watched for a long while. Nothing came close, but she was very patient, absolutely dead still, looking down towards the river where the wildebeest were crossing. And a little further along the giraffes were drinking. Occasionally one of the giraffes would turn and look at us. No one said anything.

Then quite suddenly it got dark. The African evening sun moves down quickly behind the hills and thorn bushes. The approaching dusk seemed to cover the lion, zebra, wildebeest, giraffes, and bird life like a dark grey mantle.

When we got up to the camp overlooking Lake Ndutu, we agreed that we had had an extraordinary day, right down the Serengeti: the first lion, the cheetah, the rock croppings, the kopjes, the water hole, Lake Ndutu, the beautiful, flat-topped acacia trees on the horizon silhouetted against the burning streaked sunset.

In the camp, Joshua and Richard had prepared everything — the tents, dinner, drinks. It was cool now and getting cooler. A quick shower first and then dinner around the campfire. I noticed that someone had nailed a buffalo skull to the trunk of an acacia, giving the campsite an air of African authenticity.

It had been an eventful day, but it turned out there was still a big night ahead of us. After the drinks and the dinner and the chats we turned in, and then they started... the climaxing grunts. Grunt. Grunt. Grunt. Lions, those great ventriloquists of the African wild,

A lioness is a patient hunter. Lions have keen eyesight and hunt by sound and vision rather than by smell. They almost invariably feed on herbivores, turning to man-eating only when there is a shortage of food, or if they are sick or injured.

can throw their voices across enormous distances, making you believe they're only fifteen feet away from you. "What do you think they are doing? Do you think they're coming here? How far away are they?" It was unsettling at first and quite unnerving. I remembered poor old Macomber and Hemingway's marvellous story.

> *It had started the night before when he had awakened and heard the lion roaring somewhere up along the river. It was a deep sound and at the end there were a sort of coughing grunts that made him seem just outside the tent. There was no one to tell he was afraid, nor to be afraid with him, and lying alone, he did not know the Somali proverb that says a brave man is always frightened three times by a lion; when he first sees his track, when he first hears him roar, and when he first confronts him.*
>
> ERNEST HEMINGWAY **Winner Take Nothing**

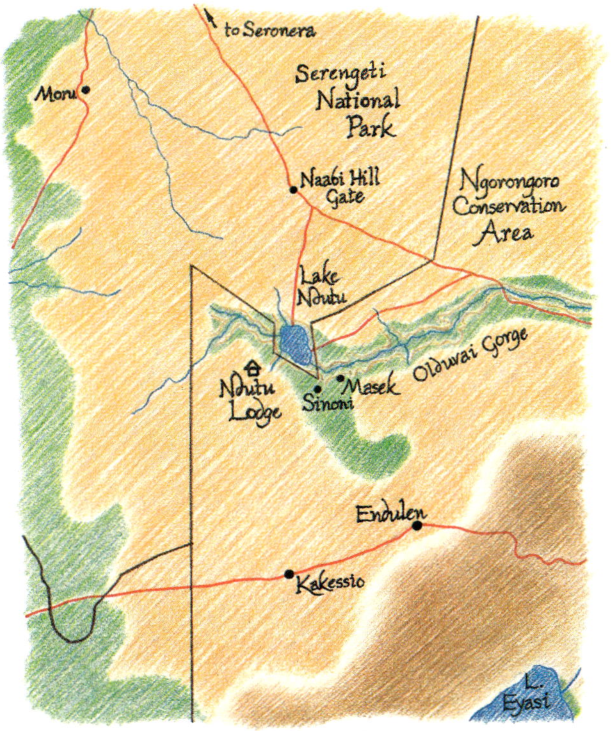

CHAPTER SIX

Lake Ndutu

But what of these lordly lazy males...? They have come in for a lot of criticism for letting the ladies hunt and then stealing the kill. It is true that the females do almost all the hunting and that the males eat their fill first, but the males play an essential and extremely important role in the success of pride life, not just by mating with the females: they also make it possible for the females to raise their cubs by providing a safer place for rearing the young.

CYNTHIA MOSS **Portraits in the Wild**

That was a great night. We did not see the lion's track but we certainly heard his roar. And not just a single roar. It lives with you the entire night. And there were other sounds — the high-pitched horse-like laugh of the zebra, the diminishing grunts of the wildebeest. Then the lions again — the roars and the coughing grunts as they called each other. Down there, no... over there. And then suddenly it seems right by your left ankle. You hear this ugh, ugh, ugh. It almost sounds as if they are making love, although they're not.

I wasn't frightened. I've never been frightened in situations like that.... Nor am I really frightened of dying. But when I'm involved in a project such as this, I'm terrified of dying before I've completed it.

Then, breakfast. I loved the African breakfasts around the morning campfire. Fruit, usually mangoes or pineapple, and a hot cereal made with either maize or the more expensive wheat. Sometimes a home-made granola instead of the cereal, and always hot, strong, black, and gritty Tanzanian coffee. A great way to start the day.

After breakfast we drove around the southern tip of Lake Ndutu, out of the thorn bush and feathery acacia trees and on to the vast, western plains. We saw hundreds of gazelles — both Thomson's and Grant's. Thomson's gazelles with their flicking

The gerenuk is easily recognized by its long neck — the word gerenuk itself being Somali for giraffe-neck. A beautiful ruddy-coloured gazelle, it can often be seen standing erect on its hind legs, long neck extended, eating the higher, tender leaves and shoots of acacia bushes and trees. It does not need to drink, for it gets enough water from its selected diet.

Previous page: Bat-eared fox and cubs.

butts, as Hemingway put it, never seem to be looking at you, always away from you. Constantly flicking, flicking. Grant's don't have the dark flash across their side.

> *I have seen, on the plains, the gazelles play this game when I have unknowingly come upon the spot where they were hiding their newborn fawn. They would dance to you, step up before you, jump, caper or pretend to be lame and unable to run, — all to distract your attention from their young. And suddenly, actually under the hoofs of your horse, you saw the fawn, immovable... lying low for his life while his mother dances for it.*
>
> ISAK DINESEN **Out of Africa**

Farther on we witnessed the gruesome sight of a pack of hyenas, thirteen in all, feasting on the dead carcass of a wildebeest they had

Tanzania is one of the few places in the world where one can still see great herd of wildebeest, also known as gnu. Their migratory route sometimes covers more than a thousand miles. They are noisy animals and their constant low grunting can be heard from miles away. Nothing can disturb the wildebeest's migratory urge. Literally thousands of these animals make their annual pilgrimage, often walking purposefully in single file, to greener fields — usually at enormous sacrifice of life.

killed a few minutes earlier. Hyenas are gruesome predators. Their sloping shoulders and wide large heads give them a hideous appearance. They are scavengers but also hunt in their own right, usually in packs. Untidy and noisy eaters, the ugly carnivores snarled and fought each other for their share, or more than their share, of their still-warm prey. The dominant females, slightly larger than the males but difficult to tell apart, ate first, keeping the smaller and weaker family members away. It was a gory sight.

Then there was the spectacle and sound of thousands and thousands of wildebeest migrating in long moving strips of black. Moving and moving as far as the eye could see in a 360-degree sweep. With their continuous grunts they sounded like a huge herd of pigs feeding. The hyenas had obviously made their morning kill from these migrating animals. The last great concentrations of wildebeest are found only in northern Tanzania and southern Kenya and they are the dominant herbivore in the Serengeti ecosystem. They are funny-looking animals, with sad faces, short horns that curve up at the ends, and well-developed shoulders and necks sloping down to weak-looking hindquarters.

The bulls, known as the clowns of the veldt, travel in herds and throw little fits, leaping into the air and flinging themselves about for no apparent reason. The females travel in separate herds, and most of those we saw were with single calves. Eighty per cent of all the calves are born during a three-week period. This is assumed to be an anti-predator reflex, as the thousands of baby wildebeest born almost simultaneously swamp the predators. The calves are up and running alongside their mothers within ten minutes of birth, but that ten minutes is crucial — the circling vultures are always hungry. It is unnerving to see them hovering and swooping to feed on the discarded fetal sacs.

Seeing the huge herds of wildebeest, it was easy to understand how hard it would be for starving Africans to resist poaching.

I returned to camp for a hot lazy afternoon. Later on, desperate for more exercise, I asked if we could do some walking. Earlier I had been warned not to go too far from camp. Lions could be skulking behind any bush. But I wanted to walk and not just be cooped up in a Jeep, so I went with Thad to a small native encampment nearby to see if we could get hold of a local guide. Individuals are not allowed to carry arms but you are allowed to go with a guide with a gun. So, with an armed guide, we walked around a nearby lake — Lake Masek. It rained through a dark overcast light that was not good for photography. It was a testing walk around the seven-mile perimeter of the lake. We once heard the short grunt and saw the shadow of a hippo. The guide with the gun was at least fifteen yards in front of us, and I kept thinking if a

Easily identified by their enormous size, black and white plumage, and red and black bill with a yellow saddle across its base, saddlebill storks are frequently seen near rivers and swamps in East Africa.

lion charged us the guide wouldn't be much help. Thad brought up the rear. We were out there all by ourselves with thick scrub all around. Then, a sudden thunderstorm. The dark rain stopped and then started again. We got quite wet, but it was a warm, refreshing rain. Instant mud and rivulets were created around the rocks. It cleared up almost as soon as we got back to camp at Lake Ndutu, leaving behind clear air and a beautiful streaked sunset that disappeared all too quickly.

At the end of the day there is a tiredness from straining — straining to use the senses. At dusk contentment steals over you. There is magic in the air, and you know that you are experiencing something quite exceptional.

I loved talking to Joshua and Richard. Joshua is the more outgoing and I had long conversations with him. Now forty years old, married, and the father of seven children, he has worked for both the Tanzanian Game Division and the Tanzanian Wildlife Corporation. Then for three years he worked for and helped various hunting safaris in southern Tanzania. Since he is of the Chagga tribe from the foothills of Kilimanjaro, his actual home is in Moshi, a fair distance away from Arusha and the Petersens' Dorobo Safaris headquarters.

> *The Chagga were and are today an intelligent, ambitious tribe of Bantu-speaking cultivators who practised irrigation in the rich highlands; like the Kikuyu, they were driven inland from the coast by northern invaders and they, too, are supposed to have displaced a small race of men with big bows and unintelligible speech, who were driven higher and higher on Mt. Kilimanjaro and eventually vanished. Subsequently, the Chagga were harassed by the Maasai and displaced by Europeans, yet later became the most powerful tribe in the country. Whether the Chagga and Kikuyu got control of the best land because they are intelligent and ambitious, or whether their intelligence and ambition is a consequence of favorable environment and good nutrition would make an interesting study.*
>
> PETER MATTHIESSEN **The Tree Where Man Was Born**

The African sun disappears almost too quickly behind brilliantly streaked sunsets against which trees and thorn bushes create dramatic silhouettes.

Joshua is indeed an intelligent, sensitive, and caring man who helped make me feel as if the Serengeti tenting life was easy and second nature to me.

I tended not to talk politics because it is a sensitive issue. Coming from an affluent capitalistic society, I wasn't going to start comparing lifestyles. But I did talk a bit about the British and the Germans in Tanganyika. It was Joshua who told me that the Germans were good settlers and quiet homesteaders. Then after the First World War, Tanganyika was handed over to the British in trust from the League of Nations. The British who came out to Tanganyika didn't really come to settle and weren't homesteaders. They had a superior attitude and treated the natives in a contemptuous fashion. By contrast, in the early years in Kenya the British arrived with their money, worked hard, colonized, and put a lot into the country. They earned what they achieved and even though they weren't always loved, they developed the country, built towns, and created commerce. In Tanganyika the English came almost too late and didn't try to develop the country. I suppose, since it was a protectorate, they never really felt it belonged to them. I had the distinct feeling that they weren't as well liked as the Germans, some of whom still live here. Many of their organizations, like the Frankfurt

Zoological Society, continue to contribute enormous amounts to the well-being of Tanzania. Germans and other Europeans still make up the bulk of the tourist trade in Tanzania, but the British, not surprisingly, tend to prefer Kenya.

Joshua spoke English quite well, but giggled a lot if asked a question. Sometimes, perhaps because he didn't understand, he walked away giggling. We talked about animals, including leopards, about which I was eager to learn anything I could. I was forever asking Joshua questions: about cheetahs and leopards and what chance we had of seeing them. How do you look for a leopard in a tree? What do you look for? What kind of tree? Sausage trees, acacia trees? What time? Morning, evening? What's the best time of day? "Well, usually they're hunting in the late evening. So they're in the trees during the day."

Notes on leopards: The leopard is the fourth largest cat, after the tiger, the lion, and the American jaguar. Slaughtered unmercifully for its valuable and beautiful skin, it is now one of the world's most endangered species. Even in Tanzania it is found only occasionally in game reserves. Very few exist in the country. A leopard has many enemies besides man, among them lions, hyenas, baboons, and hunting dogs.

Only during the mating season are leopards seen together, and after this groups of leopards usually comprise a mother and her cubs. Leopards breed throughout the year but particularly in the spring. The female comes into estrus once every one and a half to two months for about a week, and the gestation period is three months. Usually two to three cubs are born, but a litter can be as many as six cubs. The mortality rate in the young is high, and it is very unlikely that all the cubs will survive. The cubs are born in reedy thickets, caves, the hollows of trees, and sometimes in sandy dugouts. They may suckle for as long as three months. They attain their independence in a little under two years and sexual maturity in another year.

Leopards hunt almost entirely by night and are silent, cunning predators. Unlike the cheetah, which depends on its speed, the leopard catches its prey by careful, stealthy stalking. The victim is

The camp at Lake Ndutu at the southern tip of the Serengeti, where we heard the wildebeest trying to cross the water at night. Wildebeest are nervous of water and panic easily, trying actually to walk on top of it, then thrashing their way through in a completely disorganized fashion. Many drown.

usually seized by the neck, and either the neck or the backbone is broken on the ground. The prey is then either taken to the leopard's lair or carried up into a tree, where it is wedged in the fork of a branch.

Only very occasionally do leopards hunt and spring on their victims from trees. However, they are superbly proportioned and can leap at least thirty feet towards a victim. They have also been seen to leap more than ten feet vertically.

The night noises again. A symphony of night sounds. The birds stop singing when darkness falls and a different world comes to life.

The unusual hyena laugh is an eerie sound that can be terrifying, especially at night. It is generally a signal that the hyena is mating or excited. But the low moaning wail rising to a high scream can be heard throughout the night. Their powerful jaws and teeth make hyenas among the most feared of all the carnivores.

Lions usually sleep in the day and hunt by night, grunting and growling and coughing and spluttering. The occasional shriek of a zebra. We heard the wildebeest going across Lake Ndutu again with their hoofs tripping through the water. In the morning we could see that the odd one had drowned — there were hoofs sticking up in the water. It was a night very much like the one before and we didn't get any more used to it. We never did.

I awoke at 1:00 a.m. to the sound of a hyena sniffing at the head of my tent. It was separated from me by the thin nylon fabric, but it was only a few inches from my face. Although I kept telling myself that there was no real danger, I couldn't help imagining what those strong jaws could do with a single savage bite. I had already seen the vicious carnivore in action. I could smell it, too, with its damp fur. A putrid stench. Although it moved away after only a few minutes, I had an uneasy time of it.

This set the stage for another night of drama, when a whole pack of hyenas chose to invade our camp. They were everywhere, moaning, wailing, grunting, and occasionally snarling at each other. We listened to them on and off for the next three or four hours. Finally the noise became unbearable, climaxed by one ambitious hyena which climbed onto the large metal food containers piled on the camp table, and collapsed with them in a tumbling clatter on the ground. Joshua got into the Jeep, turned on the lights and found that no fewer than a dozen animals had gathered around the food boxes. Even when he turned on the engine they were reluctant to leave. He finally dispersed them by driving around them and pushing them away with the Land Rover. They returned half an hour later, but after one more attack with the Land Rover they disappeared for good, wailing discontentedly into the night. We had perhaps two hours' sleep. Joshua told me the next morning that when he shone his torch on the scene there were eyes everywhere.

When we got up, it was still dark. I was half asleep and Joshua's strong coffee was very welcome. The fresh fruit, cereal, and Tanzanian coffee are all part of the daily routine. Nothing is said. They are just there: fuel to start our daily journey. We were going to get out early that morning to see wildlife at work. The best times are just as the sun comes up and in the evening just before the sun goes down. That's when predators hunt and feed.

The morning was still. There was no wind and no sound and it was too early for the dawn bird chorus. In the soft pre-dawn light we looked out over the mud flats and the lake and saw in silhouette a solitary male lion, no doubt one of last night's grunters. We watched him through binoculars and photographed him for about a quarter of an hour while he plodded purposefully along the lake-shore as if going to some appointment at the other end of the flats.

Just as the sun came up we saw an agitated cheetah, very disturbed and looking at something — we didn't know what. She was worried, looking back and from side to side. Most predators can take food away from a cheetah. Even a hyena, and sometimes vultures. We presumed that some predator had stolen the cheetah's early kill and that the cheetah, still hungry, was looking for something else to hunt.

While we were watching and hoping to see the cheetah rush and kill, over on the other side of the hill we noticed a lioness slowly stalking up the valley along a hedge of saltbush. She was

Certainly the wildebeest is rather a pathetic effort. He is a sort of sham — he looks so fierce and is as mild as a sheep; he seems built to charge, with his humped shoulders, and thick neck, yet I believe he is never known to do such a rude thing. He is so quaint that you feel he ought to be rare....

MARGERY PERHAM **East African Journal: Kenya and Tanganika 1929–1930**

quite far away, perhaps a hundred yards, and intent on her pursuit. "I think she's hunting. I really do think she's hunting." We stopped watching the cheetah, which I was loath to do, and moved closer to the crest of the hill to get a clearer view of the lioness without disturbing her. Now we were only sixty or seventy yards away.

We moved even closer, perhaps to within fifty yards of her. She was half crouching, stalking something very slowly and stealthily. Quite suddenly a lone wildebeest appeared, going up the little valley, fifty yards ahead of the lioness. Then, I don't know why, the wildebeest, a medium-sized thing, perhaps a year old, turned almost sharp left and came over the crest of the hill, away from the cover and out into the open to within twenty or thirty yards of where we sat silently in the Land Rover.

As it came across it was actually cutting short the distance between it and the approaching lioness, although across the bottom of the hill the wildebeest couldn't see her. We knew that the likelihood of seeing a lion kill was small. Nevertheless a lioness stalking alone is a wonderful sight.

Then in one great rush, the lioness was on the wildebeest, grabbing it around the neck with her claws, bringing it to the ground and suffocating it with a firm grip of her jaws on the wildebeest's windpipe. For well over a minute she stayed in this position, absolutely still. Then after furtively looking to left and right, checking for other predators, she dragged the carcass into the nearby bushes with an amazing show of strength. She pushed the dead animal forward between her forelegs rather than dragging it backwards. She ripped the stomach open and ate the entrails first. We drove closer, clearly annoying her, but not enough to drive her away. When she had had her fill she left the carcass in a gory state. There was blood all over her face.

The original male lion now appeared on the scene, put on a brief show of stalking the dead wildebeest, and then inspected the kill. This was a full fifty minutes after we had first seen him half a mile away. The old warrior clearly knew what he was doing. Once the female had moved away, he dragged the remains farther down towards the lake and hid them in a clump of dense saltbush. During the half-hour we watched him he didn't eat any part of the body, obviously intending to save his feast for a later time. On our drive back to camp we saw our lioness, who had by then cleaned herself and had been joined by another lioness. Both were lying unconcernedly and contentedly in the morning sun.

The circle closed. It was as if the male had made a plan earlier in the morning and it had been carried out successfully with the

Although the lioness kills more often than the male, the lion invariably participates in the feast once the kill has been affected. Hunting is done in either the late evening or the early morning and the prey consists of a great variety of animals, including wildebeest, zebra, hartebeest, gazelle, and antelope. Larger animals like the giraffe and buffalo are usually hunted by groups of females. Only one in nine hunting attempts is successful.

full understanding of the two females. We were lucky to have seen it. Thad told us that it was the first lion kill he had seen in almost a lifetime spent in the bush.

When you first get to Africa you presume that you will side with the hunted rather than the hunter. Quite the contrary. You soon find that all your predatory instincts come out and you are totally on the side of the predator. You are the hunter, and I defy anybody to suppress that natural instinct. You want to see the kill and you want the kill to be successful.

On the way back to camp we witnessed another kill on the mud flats next to the lake. This time a solid mass of vultures clawed for position while devouring a tiny wildebeest calf. Towering over them stood a pair of marabou storks. Two Nubian vultures with massive bills and purplish-grey faces swooped down and at once established a superior position but only until we moved the Jeep closer. More nervous of us than the others, they then relinquished control to the smaller but less nervous Ruppell's vultures. A white-backed vulture, oblivious of its audience, kept on tearing flesh. All croaked and squawked noisily, greedily squabbling and hissing among themselves for their individual rights.

White-backed and Ruppell's vultures are adept at pulling out large pieces of meat from the dead carcasses of animals, while hooded and Nubian vultures tend to pick meat directly off the bones with their sharper beaks. Although principally scavengers, vultures do kill their own prey — particularly new-born wildebeest and gazelles. Marabou storks are often seen towering over the kill, greedily participating.

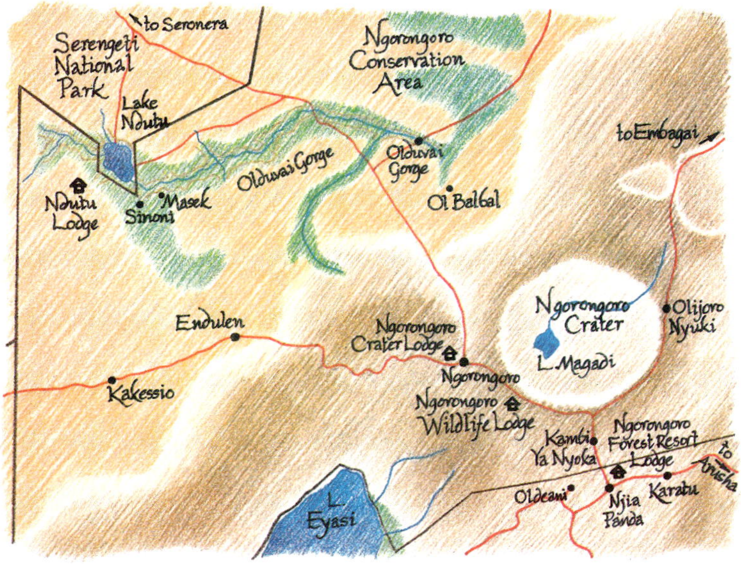

CHAPTER SEVEN

Ngorongoro Crater

Ngorongoro is a great steep sided caldera, a collapsed volcano, and it constituted a formidable obstacle on the road from Arusha to the Serengeti Plains. The route by which the lorry and we ascended had only just been made. It was a track, through forested country, which clawed its way to the top in a series of hairpin bends before running along the narrow rim of the huge crater itself.... This is now my regular route to Olduvai....

MARY LEAKEY Disclosing the Past

We left Lake Ndutu within an hour and headed for the Ngorongoro Crater, leaving Joshua and Richard to pack up. Our route took us a long thirty-seven miles south through the dustiest, driest corner of the Serengeti to the famous Olduvai Gorge, which really should be *Oldufai*, the Maasai word for the wild sisal that grows around the edges of the gorge.

It may be that man's earliest ancestors lived in the gorge. Fossil bones of the Australopithecus or Zinjanthropus Man have been found there. The gorge was accidentally discovered in 1911 by a German butterfly collector, Professor Kattwinkel. Quite by accident he found a very early fossil bone, which he took to Berlin. A further expedition to the gorge was made in 1913 by Professor Hans Reck, who returned to Berlin with more fossil samples.

Twenty years later Louis Leakey led a fully organized expedition to Olduvai that included Professor Reck and Leakey's wife, Mary. Louis Leakey found very early stone tools of ancient man on the very first day of the expedition only a few yards from their campsite. However, it was not until Mary Leakey unearthed the skull of the Zinjanthropus Man nearly fifty years later that the world realized the importance of the Olduvai site and the archaeological work of the Leakeys.

It is clear now that there existed two types of early man at Olduvai: *Australopithecus-Zinjanthropus boisei*, and *Homo habilis*. The former was referred to as the Nutcracker or Handy Man, while

Hippos threaten other hippos by opening their jaws wide to show the inside of their mouths and their teeth. Males bite each other often. Hippos are herbivores and can eat over a hundred pounds of plant material during a single night.

Previous page: Zebras and flamingoes in the Ngorongoro Crater.

The sacred ibis, once worshipped by the Egyptians (and sacrificed and mummified by the thousands), is still a familiar sight in East Africa.

the more intelligent *Homo habilis* was probably the direct ancestor of modern man. *Homo habilis* made and used stone tools and lived in primitive shelters. He was a meat-eater but did not use fire. It is interesting that one of the most recent geological formations in the earth's history, the Rift Valley, also contains the earliest evidence of man's history on earth.

We stopped for lunch under a solitary acacia on a promontory looking out over the southern Serengeti and then drove the remaining twenty-four miles to the Ngorongoro Crater. Leaving the dust of the plains, we climbed the rim of the crater, passing through many changes of vegetation, and then, in a wonderfully golden yellow sunlit afternoon, descended the steep rim.

The slender, pink legs of the black-winged stilt make this African winter visitor easily recognizable in the inland lakes and marshes.

Eight million years ago Ngorongoro was an active volcano. When its core collapsed, it left one of the biggest craters or calderas in the world. Almost nine miles across, twenty-five hundred feet deep, and covering over one hundred and two square miles, the crater is one of the wonders of the world and one of the most spectacular game haunts in Africa.

We entered by the Lerai Descent, an extremely steep winding track down the slopes of the crater wall. Below us the open grassy plains with lakes, swamps, and patches of dense acacia woodland presented a breathtaking spectacle. Game was everywhere, and we were to have one of the most fascinating afternoons of our entire safari, though not without danger.

Of all the creatures, none dressed so well as the birds of Africa. They had summer and winter dresses, special silks for making love, coats and skirts for travel, and more practical clothes that did not show the dirt and wear and tear of domestic use.

LAURENS VAN DER POST **The Heart of the Hunter**

The bird life was incredible. I took countless pictures of Hottentot teal, sacred ibis, avocets, spoonbills, herons, harriers, and crowned cranes. As we were pursuing a pink band of flamingoes on one of these central lakes, we disturbed, very close to the track, a serval that was clearly hunting. The beautiful tawny-yellow, black-spotted serval is only forty-eight inches long and has a short black-ringed tail eight inches long. It has long legs and large oval ears and can and did disappear quickly in long grass. We were patient. The intent cat changed position and location a number of times, always looking for its kill, but was not successful.

The delicate, long-legged serval cat is extremely shy. It is seldom seen during the day and then only near marshy country.

It has also happened that a male rhinoceros has sometimes assumed a car to be a female rhino (they are very short-sighted) and, after walking slowly round on a tour of inspection, has become very angry on discovering its mistake.

BERNHARD GRZIMEK **Twenty Animals, One Man**

We also saw and photographed a black rhinoceros and her calf, and then another pair of females. It is tragic that these almost extinct animals are being butchered by poachers for their horns. Unless they can be kept in protected areas, their chances of survival are slim. Rhinos have good smell and hearing but poor sight. They weigh more than a ton, are solitary and bad tempered, and will charge anything, including a Land Rover. We kept our distance.

Great herds of zebra were scattered across the crater floor, and we watched one making a fool of itself rolling in the dust. Zebras look like comfortable, overstuffed ponies, and they certainly appear to derive a great deal of pleasure from rolling in the dust and dirt. They are very sociable and live in small herds of usually about eight

to twelve members, although enormous herds sometimes numbering in the hundreds are seen during the migration and dry seasons. They never stray too far from water holes, and their unique high-pitched bark is one of the most stirring sounds in the African wilderness.

Two male lions sprawled in the hot afternoon sun, and later a pride of four females lurked lean and hungry and yet dangerously playful. The females would do some hunting later that night.

On our way back to camp an enormous bull elephant with exceptionally large tusks loomed above us, too close to the track for us to risk passing him. We stopped and waited patiently while he watched us. Then, when he started to move towards us, Thad couldn't start the Land Rover. It was a terrifying moment that stretched to a long ten minutes. The elephant walked towards the Jeep and drank water from a pool on the road only a few feet away. He then stood and watched us some more. Again the Land Rover wouldn't start. Finally, after what seemed an eternity, he ambled away to the side of the road. We remained very still and quiet, praying we would not anger him in any way. On our third attempt the Jeep did start, just, and we made our way around the enormous bull to safety and to our camp. I admit to some degree of fear. Anything could have happened. Thank God the crater elephants are somewhat accustomed to cars and Jeeps. It would have been a different story in Tarangire where the elephants are much more hostile.

The fact that camp was only a few yards away from where this encounter happened didn't make us feel particularly secure. I was badly in need of a bath and had a freezing cold shower, uncomfortable at the time but invigorating. We had pilau for dinner and the conversation was lively. Many elephant stories were exchanged in Swahili, some of which Thad translated, and some of which Thad told. A few months ago in the Mikumi Reserve, one poor tourist, seeing a large tusker in his camp when he got up in the middle of the night, thought it the right time to get a flash photograph. He was trampled to death.

The African elephant has learned to hate and distrust man to such an extent that any encounter with this largest of land mammals involves a considerable amount of danger. Much of the male elephant's time is spent alone, or else they have small herds of their own and stay away from the matriarch and her family unit. Males tend to join female herds only when one of the females is in estrus.

Hyenas tear their prey to pieces, then scatter it in all directions, preferring to eat in solitude and not side by side. They are known to practise passive cannibalism: if a hyena has been badly injured, usually by its prey, other hyenas may devour the injured one in the mêlée of the initial feasting.

The heat of the day gave way to a cool evening and a cold night. I went to bed with a sweater and a blanket and was having difficulty sleeping when the night was made hideous by a sound that began with a soft groan and rose with repeated short calls to an ear-splitting climax. I thought some appalling murder was being committed just outside the tent. It was in fact a tree hyrax. These small mammals look like guinea pigs but are hoofed. They habitually make an awful noise to mark their home range late at night and very early in the morning. They are herbivores, and seem to spend most of their time eating and screaming.

I remembered an occasion when I was camping with some friends from Europe. It was about three hours after sunset and we were sitting around the campfire. Earlier we had heard lions roaring and hyaenas giggling hysterically, but for the past hour it had been almost silent

except for the sound of crickets. Apart from the small circle of light created by the flickering flames of the fire, it was pitch dark. Suddenly, a few metres away and without warning, the most blood-curdling screams shattered the silence. My friends froze in horror. I can only describe the sound as being like the cry of a pig being slowly throttled. In fact it was the healthy call of a little tree hyrax, seeking a mate or proclaiming its territory.

HUGO VAN LAWICK **Among Predators and Prey**

Hyenas too made a night of it, howling eerily around us and punctuating the restless night with hungry calls. We could hear their heavy throaty breathing, and they padded noisily around the tents, unlike lions who are silent when they walk.

We got up very early. It was cold. I had on a sweater and my leather safari jacket. Thad had on one of his parkas. I was glad to be wearing my hat, to protect me not from the sun but from the cold. I had forgotten that we were seven thousand feet up. It warms up only gradually in the crater, and the morning light is yellow and not nearly as beautiful as the warm, soft, tangerine light of the evening. The sun is slow to appear over the rim of the crater, but then

assumes its customary harshness very quickly.

If I could stay in Africa for an extended period I would study the hyena. Its very repellence is fascinating.

Hyenas eat not just the flesh of their prey but all the bones, too, and consequently their dung is white and chalky. Fearless when hunting in a pack, they are much more dangerous than they appear and wouldn't hesitate to kill a human if he was weak and vulnerable. That's why I didn't feel totally at ease when sleeping in a small, thin tent with hyenas around.

> *...the hyena has taken...female liberation to an unexpected conclusion. Somehow in its evolution the female hyena has developed external genitals that are exactly the same in appearance as the male hyena's: her elongated clitoris is the same shape and size as the male's penis, and she has a sham scrotum...she is both larger and stronger than the males and dominant in the hyena social system.*
>
> CYNTHIA MOSS **Portraits in the Wild**

Driving to the eastern edge of the massive crater we saw little game until we spotted a lion and lioness some distance away. Approaching cautiously we didn't have long to wait, perhaps ten minutes, before they mated. Snarling briefly the lioness summoned her big mate. A few seconds later, with snarling, biting, and a final cuff from the female, it was all over. Near a pride but a little apart from them we saw yet another pair of mating lions. When lions mate the female calls the tune. Again the lioness snarled her inviting command before the male mounted her and quickly reached his noisy climax. The after-scene created further drama. The two rolled away in a semi-exhausted state, but a second male thirty feet away sat upright and attentive. He was there ten minutes later while the mating lions slept, obviously waiting in case the loving male was tired and he could replace him in his duties. Lionesses allow this, but they don't usually change partners unless the first partner tires or leaves.

One of the most beautiful animals in Africa, the impala has a bright fawn-coloured coat that seems to blend perfectly into its environment. Unlike the Thomson's and Grant's gazelles they tend to stay away from the open plains and are usually found in denser habitat.

Towards the beginning of the lions' mating period the female will usually walk in front of the male, flicking her tail in his face, rubbing against him, and generally giving him her scent. When she has crouched the male will mount her, snarling and growling, and bite her neck. After a few thrusts and in a very few seconds, it's all over. The two snarl at each other and she will often cuff him before he dismounts. At the beginning of their courtship they will repeat this routine every fifteen minutes or so. However, towards the end of their tryst the time between mating lengthens to as much as an hour. A courting pair stays together for the better part of three or four days. Neither the lion nor the lioness eats during the whole period!

Shortly afterwards we came across four lionesses hunting and stalking a small herd of buffalo. We stopped and watched them. Unfortunately they were up-wind of the spread-out herd of buffalo, and when two of them had stalked their way to within twenty yards of the herd, the wary buffalo got their scent and moved quickly away from them. It was nevertheless a fascinating study in organized and patient hunting skill. Hardly moving, the lionesses crept purposefully forward in perfect formation towards their quarry.

Here in Ngorongoro where there is such a density of different species living close together, the relationship between the animals — including predators and their likely prey — is oddly easygoing. Lions laze around with zebra and wildebeest in close proximity. The Thomson's gazelle grazes happily, twitching its tail, within yards of a pride of lions. The hunted know when to be careful. They sense when the predators are hungry.

We moved on away from the eastern edge of the crater towards the central lake, looking for predators and hoping to see a morning kill. We were too late, but we did come across the almost eaten carcass of a recently killed zebra on which three lionesses had been feeding. One female walked away, presumably satisfied, but the other two remained, protecting their respective portions of the dead zebra, snarling, gnawing, and eating whatever meat they could glean. We were very close — closer than we had been to lions at any other time. As a result I got some very close character photographs at a kill. A sensational and gruesome experience.

Later in the morning we found a herd of thirteen hippos wallowing in a pool — a large male and several females and young ones, who gave us an entertaining half hour.

> *By and large the hippopotamus is a harmless beast, unless you scratch his submerged back with a canoe. Hippos can weigh up to three tons, reach a length of 14 feet, and have reddish sweat. They can stay under water for about four minutes, and sometimes for brief intervals they walk on river bottoms completely submerged. Natives like hippo fat, which is used as a substitute for tallow and grease.*
>
> JOHN GUNTHER **Inside Africa**

Opposite page: A lioness and zebra carcass in a morbid embrace.

Few lions will attack men unless they are goaded into it; most buffaloes will. A lion's charge is swift and often fatal, but if it is not, he bears no grudge. He will not stalk you, but a buffalo will. A buffalo is capable of mean cunning that will match the mean cunning of the men who hunt him.

BERYL MARKHAM West with the Night

These huge river horses spend most of the day submerged in water up to their nostrils, surfacing occasionally for a yawn. They come ashore at night to feed on grass. Despite their enormous bulk they can easily outrun a man.

A large herd of buffalo grazing nearby threatened to charge if we got closer. Buffalo are the most aggressively dangerous of all the African big game.

As we left the crater I marvelled at it once again. Looking down, it was difficult not to think that we were leaving some special kingdom. The hawks and the eagles hovered above us as I turned back for another glimpse. I could see in the distance the little dust storms and the shimmering light over the crater floor — another world — miles below us.

On a new summit track we circled the south-east rim for fourteen miles through thick, high-altitude acacias to the south main road that winds down to the Oldeani Valley. It was a new drive for Thad and a breathtaking one for me. On one side rose dense rain forest, while on the other was a precipitous drop to the crater floor. The views were unbelievable.

We stopped for a moment by the monument to Michael Grzimek and six others who had given their lives in the study and protection of wildlife in the area. Then we reached the clay main road — what a relief to get back on something more navigable! — and descended quite quickly into the lowlands and farmlands of the lush Oldeani Valley. We climbed again first through bean fields and then through coffee plantations to Flycatcher's Farmhouse. At one time a plantation manager's headquarters and now a lodge, the idyllic retreat was managed by David Bygott, a well-known photographer and field artist, and Jeanette Hanby, a naturalist.

I couldn't help thinking about Karen Blixen and her early life in Kenya. Her coffee farm had been too high. She had been warned it was too high, but tried to make a go of it anyway, with eventual disastrous financial consequences. Here in the Oldeani the coffee was doing well — luxuriant, extraordinarily bright, shiny green leaves. The lush greenery was wonderful after all the dry red dust. The coffee bushes stood so high on either side of the estate road that we couldn't see over them. I grew up on a tea plantation, so I remembered the rolling green landscape well, but after the dusty plains I hadn't expected such luxuriant tropical colour. Coffee is grown on steep slopes, as it needs good drainage, so the view from the farm looked down an endless valley.

It felt strange to stay in a house again, to encounter an organized garden, clean sheets, chairs, walls, furniture. However, it was a beautiful little farmhouse where you could get away from it all, clean up, and rest — an ideal retreat for Africa.

In the Ngorongoro Crater the roles ordinarily assigned to lions and hyenas are reversed. It is the hyenas, hunting at night, that make most of the kills, and the lions seen on the carcasses in daytime are the scavengers.

PETER MATTHIESSEN The Tree Where Man Was Born

The beautiful, russet-coloured Bohor reedbuck, which rarely strays far from rivers or swampy grassland, is a favourite food of leopards.

One of the Frankfurt Zoological Society researchers who was involved in a hyena project in the crater was staying at Flycatcher's for a night. He gave us a lot of interesting information about the hyena's habits in the crater. They are the dominant predators there, and their behaviour inside the crater is different from anywhere else in the Serengeti.

We had a nice dinner at Flycatcher's. By that I mean knives, forks, tablecloths, glasses, etc. I had to get used to civilized living and manners all over again. We also had some interesting conversations. Joshua and Thad swapped some of the most gruesome

safari stories. Most of the bad or dangerous happenings were in South Maasai Land and most involved lions. Joshua told us about two geologists in Selous Park who had been drinking on a hot night. One man zipped open his tent and slept with the top half of his body outside. He awoke to find a lioness standing over him. The lioness gripped his throat in her strong jaws, and when his partner eventually pulled him into the tent, he was dead.

Both Thad and Joshua told stories of how lionesses had attacked them in their respective pickup trucks. In both cases the lionesses were suckling and must have been desperate for food. The chases weren't casual. It took three separate efforts to evade three separate attacks before Thad finally got away; and in Joshua's case the lioness actually jumped on top of the tarpaulin covering the back of the truck. It took more than two miles of fast, swerving driving before she fell off. Thad's father, too, in Lake Manyara, was chased with a group of visitors in his Jeep by several hungry lionesses. They were saved only when the game warden shot in front of the charging animals. On another occasion Joshua, searching for a wounded lion, came across a Maasai woman completely eaten from the waist down. He said, and I can believe it, that it was the most nauseating and terrifying moment of his life. He didn't continue the search.

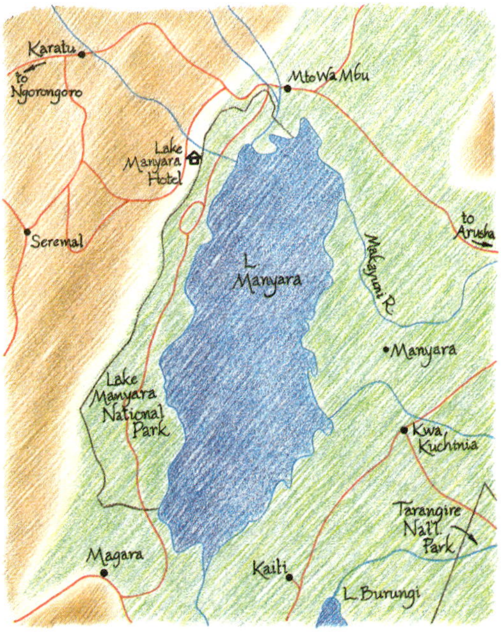

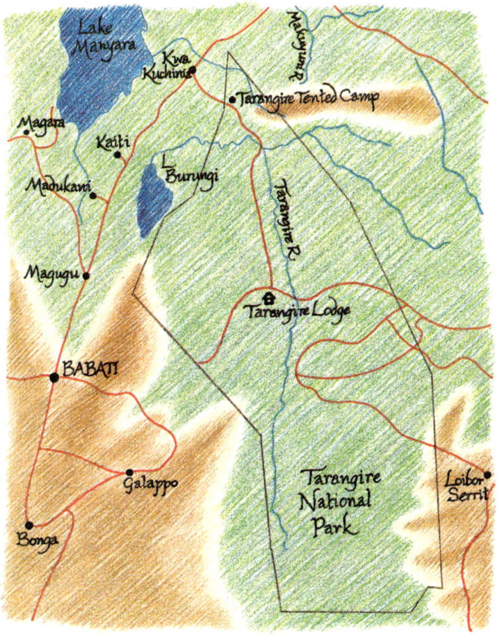

CHAPTER EIGHT

Tarangire

The African sees no more beauty or mystique in an elephant than an American does in a porcupine. For those with guns and connections, all wildlife is a source of instant wealth. For those of meager means, it is competition for the land, a marauding army that can wipe out a season's harvest in an overnight rampage.

DAVID LAMB The Africans

I awoke early in the comfort of Flycatcher's Farmhouse and lay watching the glow of dawn through the bedroom shutters and listening to the African birds and the musical murmuring of African voices. It was my birthday. Birthdays invite us to contemplate our past and reflect on our future. For the greater part of my life I had been preoccupied with achieving financial success. It had been interesting and often exciting and gratifying, but the world of complex corporate financing runs on power and profit motivation and has a limited view of what the real world is all about. To remind myself of its absurdities I read and reread the passage in *The Little Prince* by Saint-Exupéry, in which the little prince meets a businessman who has cornered the market in stars and is obsessively counting them.

"And what do you do with them?...you cannot pluck the stars from heaven...."

"No. But I can put them in the bank."

"Whatever does that mean?"

"That means that I write the number of my stars on a little paper. And then I put this paper in a drawer and lock it with a key."

"And that is all?"

"That is enough," said the businessman.

"It is entertaining," thought the little prince. "It is rather poetic. But it is of no great consequence."

The realization had begun to sink in. I had had enough of counting and banking stars. It was time for something else.

Thad wanted to have a special birthday dinner for me when we

When hunting, the secretary bird raises its inky crest like an evil halo. It consumes great quantities of rodents, snakes, and large insects. Its strange lion-like cough is heard only in the mating season.

Previous page: Elephants and baobab tree in Tarangire.

There are many different species of weaver birds found throughout Africa. This compact weaver, with its carefully wrapped bundle of a nest, is found only in Ngandu, western Kenya, and north-western Tanzania.

reached our last campsite in South Maasai Land. I told him that the only present that I really wanted was to have some more of Africa and above all to see a leopard before leaving Tanzania.

My head was still buzzing with last night's lion stories. I asked Thad at breakfast why he thought all or most of the fatal encounters with lions had taken place in southern Tanzania, more specifically in South Maasai Land. The answer was simple. Animals are more dangerous when they are hungry and there is much less game in South Maasai Land. Thus, when pushed, the large cats will go for humans.

Our route was to take us south, first to Lake Manyara and then on to Tarangire for two nights — the last opportunity for large-scale game viewing and my last real chance to see a leopard. After breakfast we drove the thirty-seven miles to Lake Manyara. Predictably, as the red clay road took us down from the heights of Ngorongoro and Oldeani, it grew hotter and drier.

Lake Manyara National Park is relatively small, covering an area of 124 square miles. The park includes the northern and most of the western parts of the lake and its shores and the westward expansion to the top of the Rift Valley. Manyara is a salt lake, like Natron, and it lies at the base of the Rift Escarpment. There are large areas of ground-water forest, with a real jungle atmosphere quite like that of the Ceylon I remembered. Giant fig, mahogany, and acacia woodlands are laced with a wide network of roads. There are also plenty

The loud cackling call of the helmeted guineafowl is often heard in the dry thorn bush areas of the Tanzanian savannah.

of open savannah spaces and tracts of scrub thorn. The air is very dry. The unusual tree-climbing lions of Manyara are famous in this area. We were going to spend the day looking for them, though we knew they were seldom sighted, and hadn't been seen in trees for nearly three years.

Soon after we started our drive into the park we saw a flock of vultures around a zebra kill that had probably taken place earlier that morning. We knew that it was a lion kill — a hopeful sign. There are no hyenas or leopards in the park. We searched the low limbs of acacia, sausage, and baobab trees in vain, and continued in other areas too, until we stopped for lunch. The Manyara lions climb trees presumably to avoid the dense undergrowth and to search for cool shade. Probably they have found they are less pestered by flies there too, for the flies — especially tsetse flies — are everywhere in Manyara.

In the midst of our concentrated search for tree lions, we were treated to a fabulous display of bird life. There are more than 450 different species of birds at Lake Manyara at different times of the year, and no fewer than 30 different species of birds of prey. We saw plenty and were kept busy searching J.G. Williams's excellent handbook, *A Field Guide to the National Parks of East Africa.*

Baboons were everywhere, aggressive and shameless, making love, jumping on the Land Rover, grabbing food, fighting. And wart hogs also seemed a lot tamer than in the Serengeti.

Baboon troops are extraordinarily well organized. They eat, sleep, and feed together, and seldom mix with other troops. A female baboon is not monogamous and will mate with any male in her troop. The gestation period for baboons varies between 150 and 200 days, and usually one infant is born — very occasionally two. The little baboon babies are in great demand and are fondled, caressed, and carried by other members of the troop. Babies often ride on their mother's back like jockeys.

The day grew hotter and drier. We found a shady place for lunch and rested from our lion search. Baboons surrounded us, and we were amazed to see how possessive the older baboons were of the babies. After lunch we drove endlessly looking for tree lions. Another large herd of African buffalo grazed on the plains near the lake. There was anger in their eyes when we came close. They always turn to face their enemy, taking their threatening stance — a menacing beast with only a single enemy: man. Two hours later, tired and dehydrated, we called it quits and headed for Tarangire.

The search for tree lions had been fruitless, but it was a wonderful

day for photography: wart hogs suckling, zebras drinking, hippos yawning, baboons fighting over babies, buffaloes threatening to charge, and birds simply showing off their colours.

Tarangire is about fifty-two miles from Lake Manyara, and the road to it on the Manyara side is very bad. We took a short-cut through the former estate of an Englishman who had got on the wrong side of the law and been murdered. His vast, arid savannah lands where giraffes and wart hogs graze are now owned by the government. The seldom-used tracks across the region are appalling. We gambled once and crossed a steep muddy river with very soft banks. We won; but when we tried to circumvent a rutted part of the old estate road we lost and got a flat tire. I am glad we didn't get stuck in the river instead!

Tarangire is only 69 miles from Arusha, and the park's boundary engulfs a 10-square-mile area with low-lying hills to the west, south, and east and the Tarangire hill in a dominant central position. The Tarangire River runs through the park, and during the dry season, from June to October, this river is the life blood of the animals. The Tarangire eco-system is similar to that of the Serengeti, and the main migration starts at the beginning of the short rains in October and November.

Wildebeest and zebra are the first to move, followed by elephant, gazelle, buffalo, eland, oryx, and hartebeest. They disperse to the north and south, most settling in Lake Manyara, Lake Natron, and Mkumgero. They remain dispersed throughout the long rains in April and May, but when the Maasai plains begin to wither at the start of the dry season in June, the animals, again led by the wildebeest, come back to Tarangire. That is when the area is really in high season — when it is dry. They remain until the rains come again in October, and then start to move all over again.

Tarangire has a character all its own. Because of the presence of the tsetse fly, it has few tourists and feels remote and peaceful. Impala, giraffe, kudu, wart hog, and bush buck are permanent residents and remain behind when the other animals migrate. There are also big herds of quite wild and angry elephants, and the occasional leopard and cheetah are also seen. The bird life is always varied.

Of all the antelopes, the impala is the most visually satisfying. It is impossible to tire of seeing it — its soft brown eyes, its velvet coat, its grace and lightness of movement. The female impala will only breed with a male that controls a territory.

There are more elephants in Tarangire than anywhere else in Tanzania. Realizing that their best protection against poachers is to band together, it is not unusual to see herds of over a hundred elephants in protective formation.

Later in the afternoon we set out to drive around the park. The landscape here is like the Serengeti, a savannah with huge baobab trees, acacia trees, low-lying bushes, little valleys, and dry river beds. The baobab trees are everywhere, all scarred and tortured by elephants. Practically every baobab tree in Tarangire has been brutally marked by them. They dig into and peel away the bark searching for juicy pulp to eat. Eventually the trunks become too weak to hold their top-heavy branches and fall and die.

Only the centuries-old baobab trees emerge unscathed by time and remain as indomitable evidence of the natural progress of the fallen seed. Noble and stripped of leaves for the best part of the year, the gigantic trunks are pitted and scarred, gleaming silver in the morning then purple as the day ages in the westering sun. Swahili legends claim that the devil himself up-turned the trees in a rage, daring them to survive the indignity of his leaving their roots, which God would have protected within the dark womb of the soil, exposed in contrast to the punishing sun. There is a sarcasm in the shape of a baobab which produces a grotesque yet fascinating beauty. Their leaflessness defies their Luciferous penalty.

Errol Trzebinski **Silence Will Speak**

Leopards often take their victim into the high forks of trees where it is safe from other predators, and the remains of this gazelle carcass on the outlying branch of an acacia tree in Tarangire signified a leopard kill.

It is ideal leopard country. It was tantalizing to see almost immediately in a tree a gazelle carcass that had obviously been put there and partly eaten by a leopard. But no leopard.

There are more elephants here than anywhere else in Tanzania. We came upon a herd of at least a hundred of them in a long single file watering themselves and rolling in a mud pool. We returned to them later in the evening and this time disturbed the herd. The adult elephants formed a protective circle around their calves and made sham charges and other threatening gestures, spreading their ears wide, lifting their trunks, and trumpeting. The matriarch was dominant both in leading the herd and in making the threats.

When I was out alone the following day with Thad, we found another herd of females with a solitary bull and a baby calf. Thad's technique in approaching the elephants in the Land Rover was one of cautious aggression, rather like that of the elephants themselves. He would drive straight up to them and stop, not seeming to react at all to the sham charges but keeping the jeep in gear and with the clutch in the whole time in order to make a quick getaway if necessary. I knew, and he knew, that we were too near. This time they were genuinely annoyed, and one matriarch with her ears flapping forward made a charge that was far too close for comfort, stopping only a few yards from the Land Rover. She stopped her charge using her front legs as a brake. There was absolutely no doubt in either of our minds that had she wanted she could easily have reached and mangled our vehicle before we could lurch away across the rough savannah. With gallows humour Thad coughed and asked whether I had got the photograph.

> *Elephants like to make love in the water, and take about half an hour in the process, which is noisy. This is the only animal in which the male has a heat period, and one of the few whose udders are between the front limbs, not in back.*
>
> **John Gunther Inside Africa**

I had a long conversation with Joshua about leopards, how dangerous and secretive they are and how hard they are to see. He described to me the technique of setting up leopard baits. Much of the lore and expertise of sighting the animals is a holdover from the days of hunting. First the hunters buy a couple of goats, not always an easy thing to do in a village, and transport them to an area where leopards have been seen. They then split the stomachs of the goat carcasses and drag them around to leave a scent, after which the carcasses are secured in the low branches of trees and checked briefly twice a day. Then, and only if there are signs that a leopard has been feeding from one of the baits, they build a blind nearby. At dusk the hunters must wait patiently and quietly in the blind for three or four hours. The odds of success are not good. The leopard knows they are there and is very wary.

Some years ago Joshua was on a shooting safari with a German hunter who was determined to bag a leopard. They set up baits and, after finding that one had been visited by a leopard, set up a

An elephant solicitously encouraging her sick calf. A herd is made up of a matriarch (commonly the larger and older female), her daughters, her calves, and her daughter's calves. The matriach's family may also include a single mature male and several of the matriach's sisters.

blind. They waited endlessly. The client, bad-tempered and impatient, got tired and nervous, but they stuck it out. Then, just as it was getting dark, there was a sudden, silent apparition. The leopard appeared above the carcass, looking straight at them. The client unloosed the safety catch of his rifle, making a tell-tale "click", and then stood up and shot at the leopard. The leopard vanished in a single leap. Joshua and his client jumped out of the blind and rushed around the tree in the dark looking for tracks or blood. Nothing. In a temper the German crashed the butt of his gun against the base of the acacia tree and broke it. They returned to camp in silence, the German with the two pieces of the gun under his arm. He knew he had missed his one opportunity.

The next morning, just before breaking camp, Joshua said to him, "Let's go back and look just one more time." So they went back to the blind and the tree, and Joshua got out of the car and went down the hill to see if there were any tracks or blood — and there was the dead leopard.

In his slow, philosophical and uncritical way, Joshua said,"He was a very happy man. I found de lōpard. He got de lōpard. He didn't need to break his gun."

We got up at 5:30 a.m. and after a breakfast of sugar bananas — which are much smaller and sweeter than those we get in North America — and more strong black Tanzanian coffee we drove out into the Tarangire reserve. These early morning excursions always filled me with anticipation. The landscape is tantalizingly beautiful. The air at this hour is clear, but in the distance the African mist clings to the plains as if reluctant to give way to an increasingly powerful sun. It is a moment of rare promise, as if one is about to make a self-discovery.

The sun rose, a huge red ball behind the flat savannah, silhouetting baobab trees, acacia trees, giraffe, and ostrich, until it climbed high and bright in the African sky. Also rising sharply from the plains was Mount Meru. Beyond it, a hundred miles away, the distinctive square-shaped peak of Kilimanjaro was visible, a symbol of men's yearning for adventure in Africa. I thought of my favourite short story, Hemingway's "The Snows of Kilimanjaro". In the preamble to the story, Hemingway sets a riddle:

> *Kilimanjaro is a snow-covered mountain 19,710 feet high, and is said to be the highest mountain in Africa. Its western summit is called the Masai "Ngàje Ngài", the House of God. Close to the western summit there is the dried and frozen carcass of a leopard. No one has explained what the leopard was seeking at that altitude.*

It is the tale of a writer on safari with his wealthy and too-loving wife, who has given himself over to good living and worldly pursuits. He has injured his leg, which has become gangrenous. They wait for help to arrive, but he knows it will not come soon enough. Most people I talk to about the story seem to forget the devastating and ambiguous preamble — the frozen leopard high in the mountains. Had the leopard simply gone there to die? Or had he, like the writer, really lost his way? Perhaps the leopard, symbolizing yearning, idealism and freedom — a kind of immortality — is supplanted in the end by the skulking, patient hyena for whom the dying man is no more than a promising bit of meat.

My own search for a leopard was taking on a symbolic importance for me. When I arrived in Africa I wanted to see and experience as much as I could, but now my goal and burning ambition was the leopard. At that first dinner in Arusha there came into my mind a fleeting memory of a leopard I had seen on a childhood visit to Yala, in Ceylon. I remember sitting in camp with my father, fascinated, as one of the trackers told us the story of the famous man-eating leopard of Punani, a little hamlet near Yala. Before she was shot in 1923 she had twenty human kills to her credit. Her mounted carcass was on display at the national museum in Colombo.

My ambition was now an obsession, and the extraordinary wealth of bird and animal life we were seeing, instead of deflecting me, had made me hungrier to crown it with this most fascinating and beautiful animal.

The realization that all journeys need a reason had not hit me until my conversation with Thad that first night in Arusha. There is no doubt that my search for the leopard was making the safari a more worthwhile experience for me. The fact that we hadn't seen one hadn't diminished my pleasure. As seeing a leopard became more and more imperative for me, my enjoyment of the whole safari was increasing, as if the hunt for the leopard had given everything an extra edge. The quest was making mine a solitary journey that was difficult to share. I hated to admit the possibility, but what if I didn't see a leopard?

As the day grew warmer the haze came up and gradually the

Necking matches occur only between male giraffes and can last for the better part of an hour. The sparring generally leads to one male mounting the other, but this is probably more to do with dominance than sex.

Overleaf: Giraffe love-making is at once graceful and ungainly — and not surprisingly, given the difficulties, lasts only a few seconds. The gestation period is from fourteen to fifteen months and only a single calf is born.

great Mount Kilimanjaro vanished. We searched for leopards all morning and again all afternoon along the dry Tarangire river beds and up the little tsetse-fly–infested valleys, especially in the sausage and acacia trees in which leopards are so fond of lounging. Thad and I made a trip to see the Tarangire Park Ecologist Frank Silkiluwasne to ask if he had any local knowledge, but he said that we would simply have to look hard and be lucky.

We combed the place and covered a lot of territory, seeing herds of impala, waterbuck, hartebeest, as well as baboons and the much smaller white-faced vervet monkey. The hartebeest are in greater number here than anywhere else we had been.

> *The kongoni, or hartebeest, has neither dignity nor proportion.... Everything is wrong with him. Worst of all is the setting of the head, which, especially in silhouette, looks like a distressing mistake. Add to this, sloping quarters, with the resultant ugly waddling run, and an extremely foolish expression, with nothing to compensate in beauty of colour for the undistinguished little horns, his size about that of the donkey — and you have the kongoni.*
>
> MARGERY PERHAM **East African Journey: Kenya and Tanganika 1929–1930**

In Africa all the animals fit into the landscape. The warm brown tones of the lion's mane meld beautifully with the long dried grass — wonderful camouflage. The cheetah has its spots, the impala its white underbelly coming halfway up the rib cage and the darker brown above, almost on the line of the horizon. And then there are the zebras, whose black and white stripes are hardly unobtrusive but are thought to create an optical illusion that confuses predators. All the animals, one way or another, wear a camouflage. But not the birds. For them it's "Screw you guys, we are good looking and we're going to make a lot of damn noise about it and fly around all over the place making a hell of a racket. We're beautifully coloured, look at us, we've got reds, blues, turquoise... all fantastic." It has been suggested that their showiness helps them mark their territory, as well as attract mates.

The Tarangire bird life is varied and spectacular. Crowned cranes, saddlebilled storks, ground hornbills. I don't know why, but

Certainly one of the most exquisite birds in Tanzania, the lilac-breasted roller perches on high vantage points.

we managed to get closer to the saddlebilled storks and the crowned cranes and guinea fowl here than anywhere else.

Baobab trees dominate the landscape. They are everywhere — huge massive trunks with well-leaved limbs bursting incongruously and suddenly about twenty feet from their base — as if to get out of reach of the destructive elephants, who appeared briefly on the late morning horizon slowly making their purposeful trek to some daytime grazing ground.

Later, as the sun grew hotter and higher in the hazy sky, eagles and hawks came to life and perched on the dead limbs of trees that reached like dark gnarled fingers into the heavens.

I took lots of photographs of these beautiful creatures silhouetted against the clear blue African sky. I thought often of Terry

Cheetahs, although quite plentiful in the Serengeti, are shy and solitary and therefore not easy to photograph. This beautiful, nervous cat is easily recognized by the dark tear marks running from the corners of its eyes down to its mouth.

Shortt, probably the last great field artist, who had painted many of these birds when he was in Africa. When I originally saw his drawings I thought his African subjects superb, but I had no point of reference. Now, as I looked at the creatures themselves, I had his images of them in mind, and it brought home to me more forcefully than ever what a genius he really was.

Although we saw no leopard, we did see a cheetah in the marshy plain near the camp boundary. It was an extraordinary sighting. We first saw her sitting in the short grass next to the marsh. She then slunk low and looked to be searching for prey. Two wart hogs appeared, walking slowly towards the cheetah. We watched intently, thinking we would see our first cheetah kill, but, incredibly, the wart hogs circled the sitting cheetah and then attacked her, making her take flight into the long grass of the swamp. We then watched in amazement as the three animals, led by the cheetah, walked in single file along a narrow game track into the swamp. We presumed then that the cheetah was not in fact hunting but was fully fed.

The tsetse flies were bothersome and no amount of Off or Muskol spray or oil kept them at bay. Only Thad was undisturbed, saying that the existence of the flies was merely a state of mind. The tsetse has played a major role in the land-use of the area, as it carries trypanosomiasis, a form of sleeping sickness to which domestic stock are highly susceptible. This has meant that Tarangire has not been used as a dry-season rangeland by the Maasai, and wildlife has remained undisturbed.

Waterbuck, some giraffe, reedbuck, steinbok, and one klipspringer dotted our homeward journey. We got back to camp at about six o'clock. I was glad to get out of the Land Rover, seat-weary and bitten mercilessly by the wretched tsetse flies. A cold shower refreshed my bitten body.

There was more talk about tsetse flies at dinner, and Thad told us about his father's dream. About six years ago David, Thad's brother, had been working for the government in cattle research just east of Tarangire. He came home after a six-week stint in the bush with aches, pains, and other influenza symptoms. This continued for about a week, until one night the Reverend Petersen had a dream. David was in his room, sick. All the doors and windows of the house were closed. It was a dark and still night. Quite suddenly, outside his son's window, there appeared a black face as of someone trying to get into the house and into his son's bedroom. Thad's father woke with a start and looked around the house and into his son's bedroom. There was no one there, only his son lying feverishly on his bed in a restless sleep. Back in his own bed, sleepless and worried, the Reverend Petersen thought about his dream and imagined that he, being the messenger of God, was the only one who could banish the intruder from the compound. He came to the conclusion that the face in his dream was the symbol of death.

Next morning he moved quickly. He took his son to the local hospital where they immediately diagnosed trypanosomiasis. In a few weeks his son was cured, but if he had waited even another week for treatment it would have been fatal.

Up early on our final morning at Tarangire I was desperate about the possibility of not seeing a leopard. Looking for leopards in the early morning light is very tiring on the eyes — particularly when you are standing in the back of a four-wheel-drive Land Rover, peering through binoculars, bumping along rough roads and dry river beds while being bitten mercilessly by tsetse flies. A Bohor reedbuck peered at us through the reeds, and we watched an unsuccessful zebra hunt by four lionesses who later returned to their four cubs. The zebras seemed aware of the hunters and kept their distance, constantly moving away and downwind from the predators. Six elephants slowly crossed the park with their trunks in the air in a farewell salute. We left Tarangire and set off east towards the Silale swamp, Maasai country, and Oldonyo Sambu. It took only ten minutes to drive through the gnarled and tortured baobabs for the last time. But no leopard.

Coke's hartebeest is seen mainly in Kenya and Tanzania and is certainly one of nature's most amazing caricatures. Even the inverted horns above the elongated, sad face don't seem to make much sense.

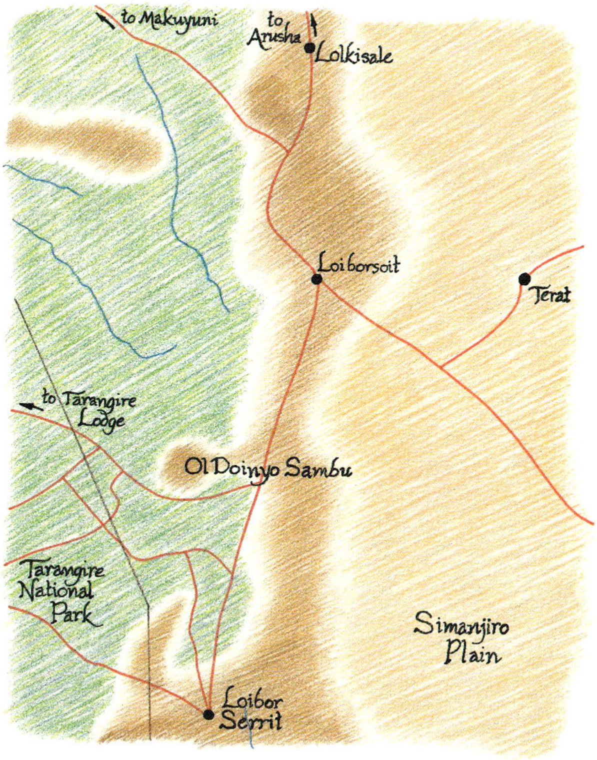

CHAPTER NINE

Maasai Country

The Masai and their cattle form part of a natural relationship to this environment. Moving from waterhole to waterhole according to season, along with the elephant, lion, giraffe, buffalo, and antelope, they were reluctant to labor and contemptuous of efforts to introduce education, which would take their sons away from herding. They required practically no money for clothing, their clothing lasting many years and never being washed.

KAREN BLIXEN **Out of Africa**

The drive from Tarangire took us into the heart of Maasai land through several villages. Just after midday we stopped in one of these villages and asked for Leure Tarmelo, a village elder and chairman of the Simanjaro Land Committee — an elected position covering six villages. We were directed to a small muddy stream, the only water supply for both cattle and villagers. The rains were late and the stream was almost dry. We found Leure on his knees trying to build a dam across the stream to make a trough for his thirsty cattle. We gave him and his most recent prize, a new-born calf of which he was very proud, a lift to his *boma*. With an enthusiastic welcome from his large family (twenty-six children and six wives) we were given sweet tea and milk — the traditional welcome to travellers. Watches, cameras, and binoculars were a source of great wonder and amusement. Children swarmed around us in the shadeless dust and dirt of the *boma*. Flies were everywhere. The Maasai hardly bother to flick them off. They are as much a part of their lives as night and day, rain and drought.

> *... in the Maasai tradition flies represent the ancestors and so it is considered an affront to brush one aside. They swarm in clusters round the eyes of the children and even the adults, and though sometimes one sees an elder with a wildebeest tail for a fly switch, as a matter of custom they accommodate to the flies.*
>
> **SIR MICHAEL WOOD Different Drums**

The Maasai are without a doubt the most purely pastoral people in all of Africa.

Previous page: Maasai women pounding maize.

The Maasai are the most distinctive and frequently seen people in this part of East Africa. Tall, thin, handsome, and proud, they have so far withstood most western influences, and cling to their way of life as warriors and nomadic herdsmen. They have not, until recently, had any laws governing agricultural land. The first British administrator in East Africa called them "Magnificent layabouts, superb to behold, but of no economic use whatsoever."

> *To the Masai ... (a) man's glory resided in his herds and flocks, and if he had no glory, what sort of man was he? As for risking the loss of them, any Masai felt himself able to defend his own against all comers, even against the Government. They would do as no man told them, only as their own sense of fitness prescribed.*
>
> ELSPETH HUXLEY **The Flame Trees of Thika**

No one knows for certain where the Maasai came from, but they are thought to have come into East Africa from the north. They probably reached the Kenyan hills, north of Nairobi, in the seventeenth century, then continued south along the Rift Valley, the Ngorongoro Crater Highlands, and eventually down to South Maasai Land and the very southern end of Tanzania. The fearless Maasai tribes met with relatively little resistance, driving the existing African tribes north and west and eventually commanding lands more than eight hundred miles long and three hundred miles wide. Their constant and ruthless raids were feared the length and breadth of East Africa, from Lake Rudolph in the north, and from Lake Victoria east to the Indian Ocean. This is probably the main reason why Maasai land remained almost unexplored until the late nineteenth century.

The arrival of the white man in Africa has resulted in a sad conflict of cultures, with the nomadic Maasai so far refusing the

Leure Tarmelo with his new calf. A Maasai elder's wealth is measured by the number of cattle he owns.

more stable and peaceful agricultural existence encouraged by western civilization.

The Maasai believe that all cattle on earth belong to them, and it is said that the Maasai warrior cares only for cattle, water, and women, in that order. But how much longer can the Maasai's freedom continue? A nomadic existence in a society controlled and driven by ownership and territorial greed seems doomed and vulnerable.

Westerners have long admired with some jealousy the bravery of the Maasai and the sexual freedom they enjoy. The comradeship that starts with the *emorata* or initiation ceremony and continues through to the *eunoto,* where the youth is confirmed as a warrior almost seven years later, is one of the strongest bonds of friendship. It continues even past the *eginasata oongiri,* or meat-eating ceremony, when the warriors are confirmed as responsible elders.

Not many people have witnessed the important initiation ceremony and not many people talk about it. After I left Africa I was lucky enough to meet and talk with a Maasai elder who described his own initiation ceremony when he was a young teenager.

He made no secret of the fact that there was a great deal of terror before the initiation. The terror is due not so much to the pain the individual is going to endure but to the certainty of disgrace if the fear becomes apparent. During the day and night preceding the initiation ceremony, there is constant talk about it and much advice. Advice as to attitude and appearance, advice as to how to stand, how to look, and most of all how to remain proud and brave. Ice-cold water, *engare endolu,* prepared by placing a metal axe head in a clay pot of water overnight, is used in a fashion similar to baptism immediately before the initiation. The initiate is dressed in black. His father adjusts his robe so that it hangs down his back before he is led, front naked, to an appointed surgeon and the operation block where he stands.

The whole procedure can be quick, but my informant's was made to last a full ten minutes. After his foreskin was pulled forward, the surgeon, with slow meaningful incisions, cut off the loose skin. After this, and quite purposefully, further incisions were made along the bottom and sides of his penis and the remaining edges of skin and loose folds were methodically cut away. He remembers not moving an inch, not stirring, not twitching his face or any other muscle, and most important of all, not making a single sound. The young initiate knows that how he behaves will be remembered by him and his family for the rest of his life.

After the ceremony there is always a great celebration for the young Maasai, given by his family and other elders of the village. A white chalk paste is applied to the initiate's forehead, cheeks, and around his eyes. The proud comrades, still keeping on their ceremonial head-dresses and white chalk paste, continue to spend time together on the plains, enjoying the great breakthrough into manhood and attending other initiation ceremonies to sing encouragement to their young friends. Whatever their behaviour during the two- to three-month healing period, it is condoned by everyone.

Encouraged to live as a single unit, the young "blood brothers" stay close together. No one is excluded from any activity, and no one involves himself in any isolated venture. In this way they are taught the beginning of their responsibility to themselves and their duty to protect their village and tribe from all enemies, both animal and human.

After the visit to Leure's village, we drove on and on through an endless herd of cattle, kicking up a cloud of dust through dense thickets. We finally reached the dry grass plains, where we disturbed

first a herd of zebra, then some ostriches, and finally a surprisingly large herd of oryx. These handsome, powerful antelopes can weigh up to 400 lbs and stand about four feet high. They are reddish-brown in colour and have beautiful black and white face markings. The female oryx grows longer horns than the male.

On to much higher land, we reached our final campsite in the shadow of a large kopje looking out over Oldonyo Sambu, a desolate area with only the occasional zebra and the odd kudu. We were all alone in South Maasai Land.

There were the same tents and the same toilet and washing arrangements. We could have been anywhere. A couple of very big rocks, a few trees, dusty soil. It was a hot dry wilderness. I noticed a lot of scorpion holes. The landscape was different in character from the denser bush of Tarangire, but the caves and clefts of the higher ground still looked like leopard country. Joshua and Richard got there ahead of us and found a leopard skull in a rock outcropping near the camp.

This was my belated birthday dinner. We all sat around the campfire eating hartebeest stew and drinking Yugoslavian wine. Thad is someone with a sense of occasion. He had sent Joshua and Richard to get me a carved ebony walking stick as a present from the three of them. They had gone to some effort to get it. Joshua also gave me his Barbaigs tribal bracelet which I have since had engraved in Swahili: "*Ametuvukiwa kwa safari* Christopher Ondaatje, Oldonyo Sambu, Tanzania, February 22, 1988." It is a very thick and very heavy well-worn piece of brass, probably over a hundred years old. It feels like gold, and I value it even more.

At the end of the evening I got one more unexpected present — a scorpion sting on the inside of my left thigh. Scorpion stings can be fatal if you are allergic to them. The wildlife photographer Hugo van Lawick, who lives near Lake Ndutu, tells an alarming story of the time his young son was stung by a scorpion. The poison ran into the boy's chest and he had trouble breathing. Van Lawick rushed him to the lodge near the lake in the hope of finding a doctor. He was lucky, and the right injection of adrenalin counteracted the poison. Now van Lawick always travels with a full medical kit.

The bravery of the Maasai is legendary, as are the bonds of comradeship that exist among Maasai youths. From their painted faces, it was clear that these sombre boys had just been through the important initiation ceremony.

The sting of the scorpion carries neurotoxins that paralyse its prey; the poison can be fatal to humans.

Thad's attitude was more casual. He did have some adrenalin but said he hadn't looked at it for two years. He got out the vial, held it up to the light and said, "It looks rather cloudy." Asked if I wanted him to inject some of it into me and if so how much, I said that I thought I'd rough it and take my chances without the injection.

It was very painful and didn't get any better as the night progressed. The poison seemed to spread down my leg in long tentacles of pain, and my attempts during the night to cool it down with applications of soap and cold water did not help at all.

In the morning I was happy to find myself still alive. Although the sting was still making life unpleasant, the pain had diminished and was replaced by a more acceptable numbing sensation. I had my leg photographed along with one of Richard's, one of Joshua's, and two of Thad's. All had been bitten at one time or another by scorpions.

We spent the morning climbing Oldonyo Sambu. The long dusty hot hike up to a series of peaks one behind the other was frustrating. We never seemed to be able to reach the summit, as there was always another pinnacle of rock slightly higher than the last. But we were rewarded with some long views across the plains. It got much hotter as the day progressed and again flies became a nuisance. On the

Elephants are hunted mercilessly for their ivory. The tusks and feet have been removed from this dead elephant carcass found in the Tarangire Reserve — almost certainly a casualty of poaching.

way down we frightened a klipspringer and then later an African wildcat. There was no sign or trace of a leopard.

The hot afternoon was spent sheltering under a large thorn acacia. A shower in the middle of a day like this is such a luxury that you feel you don't deserve it. I had one anyway. The makeshift shower that Joshua and Richard set up was actually a plastic bag filled with cold water that got hotter as the day progressed. One pulls the stopper out of the bottom of the bag and gravity does the rest.

As we slugged out the hottest part of the day under the acacia tree I told Joshua the great Kipling story of "How the Leopard got his Spots". I tried to tell him everything: the Ethiopian, the leopard, the zebra, the giraffe, the wise old baboon, the high veldt, the advice the baboon gave the leopard and the Ethiopian — and how they finally took his advice and went "into other spots".

The story, one of my favourites, tells about life on the high veldt when all animals were much the same colour — either yellowish-greyish-brownish or greyish-brownish-yellowish — with the result that, for the Ethiopian and the leopard, hunting the giraffe, zebra, eland, or kudu became a relatively easy matter. Although very one-sided, life went on until the giraffe, zebra, eland, and kudu moved away from the high veldt to the great forest area and gradually, over

Topi, among the largest African antelopes, crowd together immediately if alarmed. Highly gregarious, they live in herds of up to twenty or thirty animals.

time, changed their uniform colour to a variety of blotches, stripes, and darker lines that fitted more into their new environment. This made hunting a very different matter for the Ethiopian and the leopard, as it became extremely difficult to recognize their prey. The two hunters went to the wise old baboon, who cryptically advised them to "go into other spots as soon as you can". Not understanding the message, and getting increasingly hungry, the two hunters eventually came to the forest area where the herbivores had settled.

The Ethiopian then decided that he, at any rate, was going to change the colour of his skin so that he could hide better in hollows and behind trees. The leopard, excited because he saw the ethiopian change the colour of his skin, asked the Ethiopian to change his skin too so that it would "go into new spots".

> *Then the Ethiopian put his five fingers close together... and pressed them all over the Leopard, and wherever the five fingers touched they left five little black marks, all close together. You can see them on any Leopard's skin you like, Best Beloved. Sometimes the fingers slipped and the marks got a little blurred; but if you look closely at any Leopard now you will see that there are always five spots....*
>
> **Rudyard Kipling Just So Stories**

This final part of the story had Joshua in peals of laughter that rang across the silent Maasai plains. It was a happy moment.

Joshua then told me a Chagga fable of how all the grass-eating animals were determined to deal with the meat-eating predators that were constantly putting their lives in danger. They had a meeting. But unknown to them the lion, king of the carnivores, had word of the secret get-together. And so the lion called his own meeting at which the predators decided to send a spy to listen in to the other animals' discussion. Who was to go? The hyena immediately volunteered, saying he had a pair of kudu horns that he could tie to his head. He was sure that he would not be recognized. However, as he approached the other meeting with his kudu horns tied to his head, the giraffe, being taller than the rest, noticed the hyena and his disguise and warned the meeting of the intruder.

The wise old buffalo told his grass-eating friends not to worry and to allow the hyena to attend the meeting unchallenged. As soon as the discussion got under way, there were concerned questions as to how to stop the ruthless slaughter of the herbivores. The buffalo proposed that they should all learn to move their antlers and horns from side to side to repel attack. This was how the buffalo successfully fended off attacks. The buffalo then instructed all those present at the meeting to practise moving their antlers from side to side in an aggressive manner. This they all did vigorously, including the hyena, who found it impossible to keep his kudu horns in place for long. They fell off. He was unmasked and the grass-eaters set upon him and killed him immediately.

I listened intently to Joshua's excited narrative, which he accompanied with many hand movements. But he hadn't finished. The herbivores' meeting continued, and with great enthusiasm the wart hog suggested that a bell tied around each carnivore's neck would warn the herbivores of an enemy's approach. The suggestion was

greeted with acclaim and unanimous approval — at least until the hare raised a timid objection: "But who is going to hang the bell around the enemy's neck?"

Joshua then announced with great conviction that the hare was the most intelligent of all the animals in Africa. Though I did not mention it to him, I was intrigued by the story's similarity to the Aesop fable of belling the cat.

At dusk we drove around the dry marsh valleys near Oldonyo Sambu amid enormous anthills and thorn bushes, coming suddenly into unexpected clearings where we twice saw the scattered bones of elephants, victims of poachers. We caught a fleeting glimpse of a pair of greater kudu disappearing into the bush. They are more plentiful here in Maasai country than out in the Serengeti. Though only of medium size, kudu used to be the most prized game trophy of all the antelopes, and it is easy to see why. They are skittish, nervous, and beautiful with their lightly striped markings. The male kudu has wonderful curlicued scimitar horns.

When it got dark we used a power-beam flashlight connected to the battery of the Land Rover to look for animals. Suddenly, it was a very different world. The reflections of the eyes in the dark meant many different things.

We saw the red, round eyes of the bushbaby going higher and higher and imagined leopards scaling trees; the green eyes of the wildebeest — passive and motionless; the darting eyes of the impala leaping in alarm at the unexpected beam of light; and, most exciting of all, the eyes of the cats — bright and orange. We saw again a pair of servals with their exquisite spotted coats and short tails. They look like a cross between a small leopard and a lynx. An African wildcat ran across the plain, and we followed in pursuit until it crouched in the grass motionless, frozen. It was the same size and had the same characteristics as a domestic cat, but with vertical stripes that were barely distinguishable in the dark. Its upright ears warned that it would fight if cornered.

By nine o'clock we were ready to return. Luckily Joshua had lighted a beacon on the highest point of the kopje. Otherwise we never would have found the camp.

The African hare's sandy colour and its habit of lying motionless during the day make it extremely difficult to see. Hares are solitary except during the breeding season, when several males will stay near the female in heat.

The magnificent fringed-eared oryx can weigh up to four hundred pounds and is one of Africa's largest antelopes. Nervous and sensitive, it is most often seen in semi-desert grasslands.

We had a last dinner, tinged with melancholy. The safari was almost over.

Thad had been a good guide. He loves the outdoors and has eyes like a hawk. He recognized a Kori bustard strutting through the plains grass almost a quarter of a mile away and several times spotted lions, stalking their prey, behind long marsh grass, even though we were even farther away than the prey. He watches birds and game endlessly and tirelessly through his field glasses. Although not a keen photographer, he absorbed some of my enthusiasm and by the end of the trip he too went on a photographic binge.

Ahead lay a four-hour drive back to Arusha. Then we would drive on to Nairobi the following day to catch a flight to London. But I was not ready to leave. I wanted more time on the Serengeti.

James Augustus Grant, who made the second expedition to Lake Victoria with Sir Richard Burton in 1860, gave his name to the caramel-coloured gazelles, which usually live in small herds. A male Grant's gazelle can sometimes have a harem of up to twelve females.

I had a feeling of incompleteness, a feeling of having discovered a new world but not having secured myself in it; of finding myself in a new state of mind without knowing what to do with it; of having identified a problem without having resolved it. And I hadn't seen a leopard.

The next morning we drove back to Arusha, but my mind was elsewhere. I could not finish this trip without making one last try at seeing a leopard. The best chance of doing this was to return to Seronera. I had put the idea to Thad before breakfast, and during the long dusty drive back to Arusha I tried to persuade him to let me go back to Seronera with Joshua and the Land Rover. Thad wanted to be accommodating, but clearly he was nervous about the idea. He consulted with Joshua in Swahili, which he speaks with more animation than English. He impressed on me the likelihood of disappointment even if I did go back. "It's a long way and there's very little chance of success. At this time of year before the big rains there's even less chance." He considered the problems. He might not have enough Land Rovers on hand, and the Jeep we were using had to be serviced. What about the cost? Could he spare Joshua, and would Joshua go? Would we camp or would there be room for us at one of the lodges? Joshua pulled me aside and whispered that he knew a secret and if Thad would lend us the Land Rover he would come with me.

We had lunch at Thad and Robin's house in Arusha. I think it was Joshua who finally overcame most of Thad's objections. Joshua was eager to make the journey — his first trip with full responsibility. Perhaps because of our many conversations, he understood my need to continue my search. He was almost as enthusiastic as I. Did he know that there was more to this for me than the search for a leopard?

I wanted to get going, despite having already done four uncomfortable hours of driving that day.

> *All I wanted to do now was get back to Africa. We had not left it, yet, but when I would wake in the night I would lie, listening, homesick for it already.*
>
> ERNEST HEMINGWAY **Green Hills of Africa**

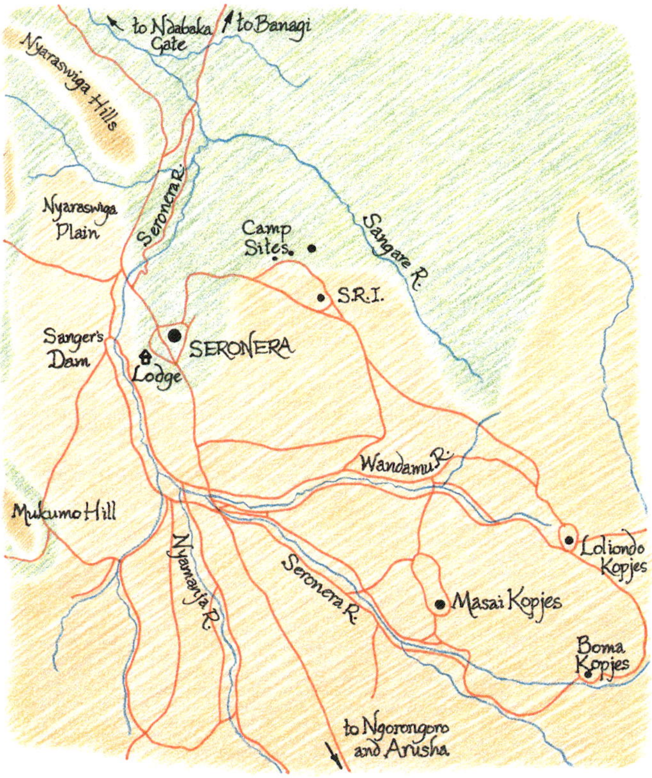

Chapter Ten

Return to Seronera and Joshua's Riddle

Come with me and I will find what you are looking for. In the shadow of the yellow fever-tree you will find beauty that you cannot touch: an image you can capture but not possess; and life you can protect but still destroy. After that you can dance to the music of tomorrow.

Joshua Mbowe

For the first few moments after I climbed back into the Land Rover with Joshua and started winding through the streets of Arusha I wondered if Thad wasn't right, if this wasn't sheer madness. But as we hit the dusty red roads and moved out into the plains I knew I was right. Even if it seemed stupid and irresponsible, it was worth making the effort, whether or not it actually paid off.

There are a few moments in life when one experiences incredible peace and happiness, and for me this was one of them. We packed the Land Rover with a few supplies and the same small nylon tents and then simply piled into the Jeep. We were off again. Out there, I told myself — where you belong. You've got a reprieve. Another couple of days. Just pushing it beyond the level of where it should be, but what the hell. A great feeling.

It was dusty, hot, uncomfortable. We could stop halfway and try to get some kind of lodging somewhere or try to get all the way to Seronera, at the other end of the Serengeti, in one go. I was as happy as I could be — willing to tolerate any kind of discomfort. It is true that the journey, not the arrival, matters.

Joshua was very keen. He knew the success of our crazy venture depended on him. He kept talking in riddles, and I kept trying to decipher them. He was exhilarated and drove recklessly. He didn't care quite as much as Thad about either the car or the potholes, and the Land Rover had a bit of a rough journey. He was also less

Joshua Mbowe drove the long dusty road back to Seronera on our final search for the leopard.

Previous page: The social organization of the topi is dominated by the territoriality of the male. Both males and females often stand on the termite mounds to see and be seen.

Our Seronera campsite was drowned in the heavy rains. But the freak thunderstorm was only a prelude to a hectic and sleepless night.

concerned about human rights and the safety of other cars or people crossing the roads — just barging on, honking his horn — and somehow they seemed unconcerned too, and eventually got out of the way. He slowed only for an African chameleon he saw in a dusty culvert on the side of the road. What amazing eyes he has!

We stopped to buy sugar bananas at Mto-Wa-Mbu, which means "Mosquito River Village" in Swahili. This is a village near Lake Manyara — a small market town with quite a history — that now sells trinkets to tourists and food for the villagers. In the old days you could buy practically anything illicit here, from ivory and skins to guns and other smuggled goods. Unpainted windowless shacks line the main road.

It is a Serengeti Park rule that you cannot enter the game reserve after sunset, so I understood something of Joshua's hurried driving. We had tried, unsuccessfully, to talk our way into the Ngorongoro Wildlife Lodge on the edge of the crater, and so had to get at least to the Naabi entrance before six o'clock. We made it, but only just, and then wound our way across the plains, through the dramatic rock outcroppings, past the giant Simba kopje, which towered a hundred feet above us, and eventually got to Seronera as darkness was falling.

Joshua seemed to know exactly what he was doing. With very little conversation we drove through the forks of the Seronera River to what I thought was a very secluded site, off the beaten track, under an acacia tree. We worked quickly and in almost complete silence pitched the two small tents by the light of a bulb wired to the Land Rover battery. After dinner Joshua told me that camping where we were was actually illegal; it was not a recognized Serengeti site. He also told me that he had camped there once before — with three nurses. The nurses had all slept in one tent on the first night, but one of them decided to separate on the second. The solitary nurse spent a fairly hectic night while an inquisitive male lion settled noisily next to her tent. The unique deep grunts and coughs terrified the poor woman, and she got no sleep. It was the last time she tried sleeping alone — on that trip anyway.

A freak thunderstorm hit Seronera that night. It was to be a night to remember. A dramatic downpour with sheet lightning started just before midnight and lasted for the best part of an hour. Then about two hours later there was another downpour, which didn't let up until 4:00 a.m. The rain heralded the real drama of the night.

The rain stopped quite suddenly and was followed by the noise of lions roaring all around the camp. We made no sound and I lay awake listening as the deep guttural sounds came closer. This nerve-racking experience continued for an hour. Then, just near Joshua's tent a few feet away I heard a single ear-splitting roar and then a scraping and flapping against his tent. Joshua screamed. I thought that the lion had attacked him in the tent, but in fact he was trying to scare the beast away. A few seconds later I heard the same scraping sound — but this time against my own tent, a few inches from my head. The lion bumped against the tent pole and rubbed itself against the tent, slinking around it. I didn't have the faintest idea what to do, but at that moment Joshua shouted to me to keep still and very quiet.

With some curious premonition, before we went to bed, Joshua had moved the Land Rover from under the acacia tree where our supplies were to the very door of his tent. It was a lucky move that may have saved us. He leaped into the Jeep, started the motor, and

turned the lights on. A lioness and her five cubs stood there. She was looking for food near the supply table. As Joshua rammed the Jeep towards them, the lioness, holding a plastic water container in her jaws, made a stealthy getaway with her cubs.

I stayed very quiet, not daring to sleep. At first light we saw what had happened. It was clear from the paw prints on the ground around Joshua's tent that the lioness had tried to attack the tent. Her teeth had torn right through the tent wall. My tent too was surrounded by her large paw prints, while the smaller paw marks of the cubs were scattered in the soft mud around the camp — especially near the acacia tree. The plastic container — quite a big one — had large tooth marks on it, and was pierced in the top corner. Needless to say, there was hardly any water left.

All this made for quite fevered breakfast talk. I wondered whether we should stay in the same campsite. I could see why it wasn't a protected area. Joshua said that he would sleep in the Jeep in case anything similar happened again. I declared that I didn't think it was possible for both lightning and lions to strike twice in exactly the same area.

Shaken but undeterred, we headed straight for the Magadi Road, which runs quite close to the Seronera River, and spent the remainder of the morning cruising slowly up the valley looking for tracks and searching the trees. The landscape looked different after the rain — more mysteriously beautiful. In the recently created pools by the river the usually sinister, hypocritical-looking marabous looked instead like solemn deacons in prayer.

In this great open brown country, the landscape is broken by shallow dried-up river valleys and by the yellow-barked yellow fever-trees, the flat-topped thorn acacias, and the sausage trees. Yellow fever-trees prefer areas near water, and early African explorers frequently camped under them because of the certainty of water and shade. Naturally, areas of water were also favoured camping grounds for the malarial mosquito. It was not known then that mosquitoes carried the malarial parasite, but people soon concluded that anyone who camped beneath the shade of the yellow fever-tree was likely to contract malaria. An association was made between some mysterious power of the tree and the fever, and hence its name.

It is in these trees that leopards usually spend most of their daylight hours. They lie in the low branches about twelve or fourteen feet above ground and are extremely difficult to see. When they move, they move under cover in long grass or dense thicket. The rougher the terrain the better, and the leopard's spotted skin provides the most perfect camouflage. Only in the afternoon can leopards be seen more easily, but it is still like looking for a needle in a haystack. You can do so only with luck or with incredibly hard work. There are tails and limbs hanging down from sausage and acacia trees all over Africa. However, most of these are imaginary, and those that belong to a real leopard usually disappear as soon as the animal has seen you.

We drove slowly along the two river valleys fruitlessly for nearly four hours, then had a makeshift lunch of bread, cheese, and peanut butter, while standing dejectedly beside the Land Rover.

After lunch we headed for the Seronera Wildlife Lodge, a sprawling complex of buildings on different levels, around and almost within a kopje. Joshua, after much heated conversation and gesticulating, managed to get us a small, single outlying room where I dumped my bags. It seemed a better bet than camping in the lion range again.

Quite by accident, we met Dr Markus Borner, the Frankfurt Zoological Society's representative in the Serengeti Park. One of the most respected experts on wildlife in Tanzania, he is the only foreigner allowed to be on the board of the Tanzania National Parks Department. Dr Borner is a pleasant, compact, no-nonsense Swiss whose specialty is animal census. I was proud to meet this well-known Serengeti character who is most concerned about the fate of rhinos and elephants — both subject to a severe increase in poaching. Very conscious that the rhino is on the verge of extinction, Dr Borner has recently made a dramatic proposal to the Tanzanian government and Wildlife Authority that all remaining rhinos in the country be transported to Robondo Island off Lake Manyara where they could be protected more easily from poachers.

Joshua then left me and said he was going to the village to try to get hold of someone he knew. I waited for a good hour, wondering what he was up to. He returned very pleased with himself and with a smiling, thick-set man in a green shirt — Martin Darabe, an Irangu tribesman from the Karatu district, a Tanzania National Parks guide who has been at Seronera for a number of years. Quiet and good-humoured, he spoke little English, but he knew the lay of the land. Joshua had obviously explained everything to him. He said our best bet would be in the early evening, about four o'clock, when leopards begin moving around to get ready for the evening's hunting. But he thought it was worth going out now, even though it was the hottest part of the day.

We had only a few hours — the rest of this afternoon and perhaps part of the next morning — so we set out and tirelessly combed the yellow fever-trees up and down the winding river valley.

Martin knew, I think, that for me the leopard was not just a simple wildlife quest and must have sensed that I was going on some other personal and emotional search too. Sometimes two people know exactly what the score is without having to say anything. He knew I was gambling a lot on him, and he tirelessly scanned the leafy horizons for us. I am grateful to Martin, and we have since become good friends.

Two hours later we were still looking. I had almost given up hope when Martin said something quietly to Joshua in Swahili, and Joshua said, "I think der de lōpard." I peered at some acacia trees and saw nothing. The leopard wasn't in the first or the second group of trees, but in the third, and very far away. How Martin saw it I have no idea. Just a tiny speck of a thing hanging down from a branch. It could have been anything.

Joshua drove the Jeep, for once carefully, keeping near cover in the rough terrain between us and the acacia tree. I looked through my field glasses and a chill of excitement went down my spine. It was indeed a leopard. A female, about five years old, Martin estimated, sprawled along the acacia branch with her four legs and tail dangling down on either side like extra branches, and her head in a fork of the tree facing us.

The fur on her belly and thighs was glistening white. Many small spots like velvet formed a bracelet round her paws; her sinuous tail was also white, ending in black rings. The back of her dress was yellow, like unburnished gold, very lissome and soft, and had the characteristic blotches in the shape of pretty rosettes, which distinguished the panther from every other species. She was three feet in height at the shoulders and four feet in length, not counting her tail; this powerful weapon was nearly three feet long and rounded like a cudgel. The head, large as that of a lioness, was distinguished by an intelligent, crafty expression. The cold cruelty of the tiger dominated, and yet it bore a vague resemblance to the face of a wanton woman.

HONORÉ DE BALZAC **A Passion in the Desert**

She seemed lazy, and was evidently quite content to spend the greater part of the day in the shade where she was. From the shelter of a neighbouring tree, and at a distance of about thirty yards, I was able to take photograph after photograph of her. Then, when I had taken every picture I could possibly take, I said, "Okay, Joshua. Now just go past her very slowly... now turn left towards her. Just go under the branch." Joshua, very disturbed, said, "I can't turn left." He was afraid the leopard would actually jump into the open Jeep. Martin was uneasy because we were breaking park rules by going off the road.

Joshua inched closer. Martin warned him worriedly not to do it, looking around uneasily to make sure there was no one to see us. Breaking the law because of a crazy guy who wants to get closer and closer. They wanted to leave. I wanted to get closer.

I had to capture that moment, and I was willing to take any risk to do so, determined to get it whatever the consequences. I was frightened, not of the leopard, but that she would leave. I kept taking shots — in case, in case, in case. Each time I got closer I thought it would be the last shot. On and on. Then I was really very close. I got out the 300 mm lens and very nearly shot her in the face. Through the lens I could almost feel her breath on me. My eyes looked directly into hers in an uncanny moment of communication. Then I took the photograph I had been looking for. Everything came together — the light was right, the focus was right, the film was right. It was a sort of love affair.

Then, almost immediately, I knew I was outstaying my welcome. It was dangerous. I'd had one of the great thrills of my life, but it was time to go. We moved some distance away, but continued to watch her. Not long afterwards she became more skittish, much more lively. She moved to a higher branch and seemed on the lookout for an evening kill. Even though we were watching her through field glasses from quite a long way away, I felt we were annoying her. We left her there.

We returned to Seronera in triumph. As soon as we got to the lodge, we headed straight for the bar for a celebratory beer — Tanzania Safari, appropriately enough. Joshua was very pleased. He had rarely seen a leopard himself, and he assured me that this was a far better achievement and experience than his earlier one with the hunter who broke his gun in a fit of temper. He and Martin went off together to the village for a more extended celebration.

The next morning Joshua told us that our leopard had been

seen earlier in the day with a handsome two-year-old male and that it was likely that they would mate soon when she came into estrus.

We had a long, bumpy, and very dusty drive back to Arusha. The winds were unusually heavy, and twice we had to drive through heavy dust storms. Visibility was often non-existent. The heavy rainstorm barely a day ago seemed almost to be a dream — sucked out of the skies and into the dry earth.

The safari was really over. I could not extend it any further, but I did not need to. I was going to miss the adventure, the dust, the taste, and the smell of Africa. And the feeling of freedom on the plains. But I recognized a new sense of resolution. Looking for the leopard had not only been a physical quest, it had been much more a journey of the mind and a search for a new life. I knew then that I would return to Africa. And I also knew the answer to Joshua's riddle.

> *When this journey out of the desert ended and the company dispersed... I discovered that in a sense the journey had barely begun. I found myself compelled to go another journey, into my own mind....*
>
> LAURENS VAN DER POST **The Heart of the Hunter**

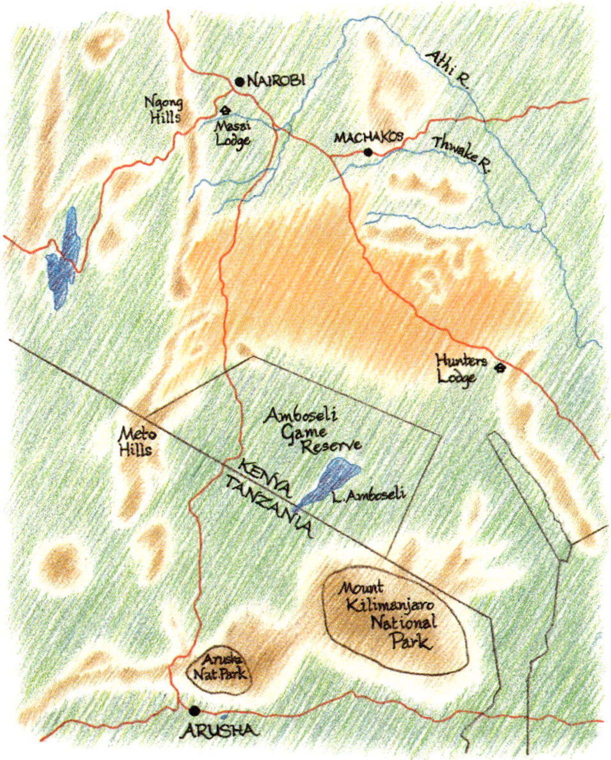

Epilogue

The survival of Africa's wildlife is for all of us a matter of great significance. These wild creatures [and] the wilderness they inhabit are not only an important source of wonder and inspiration but are also an integral part of our natural resources....

By holding our animal world in trust, we solemnly declare that we shall do everything within our power to ensure that...precious heritage.

PRESIDENT JULIUS NYERERE Arusha Manifesto of 1961

Ten months later I was back in Seronera with Joshua. This time my daughter Jans was with me. It was raining. The so-called short rains, which were to persist throughout the trip, were unseasonably late. As we huddled under the dubious shelter of a small tan nylon tent in the early African evening, I had time to reflect on the intervening months.

The tremendous release the first safari had given me, and especially the achievement of finding a single leopard in the vastness of the Serengeti, had helped me resolve the inner turmoil about my corporate and financial commitments. On the long road back to Arusha the previous February I had determined to change my life and rid myself of some of these responsibilities. I had resolved then not to return to Africa until I had made the necessary changes. I had done so, and now here I was.

On this second safari I had no pressures and no deadlines. I was able to spend a great deal of time meandering over the plains and through the valleys. The first trip had required extraordinary measures to see a leopard. But now, with no special effort on my part, the story I had started to write on that first trip completed itself for me. Quite unexpectedly, on our second day in Seronera we saw "my" leopard again. Like me, she had not wasted the intervening months. She had mated and borne two cubs. My wildlife adventure had provided its own ending and, as though by design, had given me the reason for my return.

The majesty and mystery of Africa are impossible to convey to anyone who has not been there. Many people have fallen under its spell, but it is hard not to imagine that what you are seeing for the first time is undiscovered country. On this second journey I knew much more about Africa and had a far better understanding of some of those who had written about it and whose words have become signposts to the travellers who follow in their footsteps: Karen Blixen, Ernest Hemingway, Laurens van der Post, Beryl Markham, Elspeth Huxley, Peter Matthiessen, Bernhard Grzimek. Like me, many of these writers "found" themselves in Africa. Like me, many of them sensed the fragility of its wonder and beauty.

Often, as we drove over the plains and through the small villages, I felt as if we were speeding into the Africa of tomorrow as the Africa of yesterday looked on: women digging in the fields; boys tending goats and cattle; warriors standing proudly by the roadside; young girls carrying sticks; children playing on side streets; vendors selling trinkets and beads — yesterday's emblems — to anyone not in too much of a hurry to stop and bargain.

It is difficult not to fear that everything will soon be different. We are witness to a changing world, and much will be lost in the process. Part of Africa is resisting change, but much of the society is hungry for development. There is a very real danger that the animal world will be swept away in the tide of change. The large predators have now reached the twilight of their existence, and many of the other wildlife, unless protected, may only remain as token samples of a wilderness that once existed. I am lucky to have seen it while it is still there.

Designed by Jackie Young
Typeset by PrimeType Inc.
Colour separations by One Four Colour Inc.
Printed by General Printers
on Warren's Lustro Dull
Bound by John Deyell Company